I'M A CHRISTIAN
even at work

The Ethics of Business and Economics

Jerry L. Poppe

Northwestern Publishing House
Milwaukee, Wisconsin

Cover illustration: Corbis Corporation
Art Director: Karen Knutson
Designer: Pamela Dunn

All Scripture quotations, unless otherwise indicated, are taken from the HOLY BIBLE, NEW INTERNATIONAL VERSION®. NIV®. Copyright © 1973, 1978, 1984 by International Bible Society. Used by permission of Zondervan. All rights reserved.

The "NIV" and "New International Version" trademarks are registered in the United States Patent and Trademark Office by International Bible Society. Use of either trademark requires the permission of International Bible Society.

All rights reserved. No part of this publication may be reproduced, stored in a retrieval system, or transmitted in any form or by any means—electronic, mechanical, photocopying, recording, or otherwise—except for brief quotations in reviews, without prior permission from the publisher.

Library of Congress Control Number: 2004103569
Northwestern Publishing House
1250 N. 113th St., Milwaukee, WI 53226-3284
www.nph.net
© 2006 by Northwestern Publishing House
Published 2006
Printed in the United States of America
ISBN 978-0-8100-1661-3

CONTENTS

Preface v

Introduction vi

1   Christianity as a Business Strategy 1

2   A Christian View of Economics 8

3   Equity, Efficiency, and Economics—
A Moral Connection 21

4   Christ and Capitalism 37

5   A Christian Critique of Market Economics 48

6   Capitalism and Compassion 56

7   Business Ethics: An Expression of Faith 68

8   Profits: Ethics, Money, and Business 79

9   Luther and Capitalism 90

10   Looking for the Right Answers 97

11   What Does This Mean? 148

Endnotes 152

Research Resources 166

PREFACE

For Christians, entering the world of business can be a lonely venture. The pressure to increase profits is constant. Dealing with irate customers, shrewd vendors, and demanding bosses can try our patience. As we climb the corporate ladder, we come face-to-face with the most devious and cunning of all creatures—our peers. In this environment it is easy to feel threatened and alone. And because our success in business depends on our willingness to compete, our natural response is to go down into the trenches and fight it out with the competition, using the world's strategies.

Competition often presents Christians with a dilemma. We can focus on our businesses and on our own abilities and talents to advance our businesses or our careers. Many have become rich and famous following this strategy. But we are Christians. We are different because we have an obligation, a need, a desire, and a willingness to serve the God who created us and who, after we sinned, sent his only Son to die and save us. Trusting God to direct the course of our affairs should be as natural as trusting God for good health, safety, and provisions. It's sad, but we seem to forget that. Christians in business, myself included, find it too convenient to look to God for help only with our personal matters. When it comes to commerce, we often act as if God does not even exist.

In this book we will examine how economic forces and our Christian convictions influence the business decisions we have to make. We need to understand both if we hope to make sound ethical decisions. We will use current business scenarios to examine the ethical implications of commonly accepted business practices. By studying economic theory, we will better understand how and why the scenarios develop. By applying Christian principles, we will be better able to evaluate each decision we make and determine how to improve each scenario.

INTRODUCTION

When I graduated from the University of Wisconsin in River Falls in 1985 with a degree in business administration, courses in business ethics were nonexistent. As a matter of fact, I can't remember ever discussing the ethical implications of a business decision in any of my classes. Instead, my undergraduate courses emphasized technical competence. We were taught how to use net present value to make capital budgeting decisions, how to analyze financial statements, and how to use the derivative of a cost equation to maximize profit. But we never seemed to discuss the ethical implications of the answers we found. To be honest, that never even bothered me. Perhaps because I was raised in a Christian family by parents who had strong ethical principles, I always assumed that honesty was a given when making any type of decision.

I was wrong. Corporate America marches to a different drummer than the one I was familiar with as I grew up in a small farming community. During the 12 years I spent working in discount retailing, honesty often seemed less important than efficiency. Increasing profit always was the name of the game.

Let me make it clear at the outset that there is nothing sinful or shameful about making money. Commerce has been practiced in God's creation for a very long time. The question that tugs at our Christian consciences, however, is whether we are profiting as a result of sinful business practices. Most of us can recognize that certain business behaviors—lying, cheating, and stealing—are ethically wrong. Our problem is that often the lying, cheating, and stealing are disguised as legitimate and accepted norms of business behavior. These accepted standards of business, I believe, pose some of the most difficult, yet unacknowledged, ethical dilemmas facing businesspeople. The financial statements of a firm for which I used to work provide an example.

I worked for a small midwestern retailer that was in a precarious financial position. Senior management wanted to ease the company's financial woes by raising money through a public stock offering. We were told that in order to make an initial public offering feasible, the company would have to generate strong financial results for a specified number of consecutive quarters. To meet this goal, senior management would issue the same memo a couple weeks prior to the close of every fiscal quarter. In order to meet the profit predictions given to the financial analysts, management would announce that all markdowns and expenses would be held until after the fiscal quarter had ended. In retailing, markdowns mean reducing the value of inventory to reflect the current value of the product. The greater the markdown, the lower the value of the inventory. By controlling markdowns, the company hoped to limit any negative quarterly financial results that could damage the company's stock price.

On the surface, managing expenses and markdowns does not seem to pose an ethical dilemma. Deciding when to recognize an expense is a legitimate accounting question. Managing expenses and properly reporting the financial results are fundamental responsibilities of senior management. What is disturbing is the intent implied by the decision. Is it appropriate to use the accounting system to make things look better than they really are, at least temporarily? More to the point: Are we lying? Whether we are using the accounting system honestly, and not as a tool to deceive investors, is not always clear.

Failure to appreciate the ethical implications of a business decision is a problem that is not confined to people working in business. I was surprised to find out how little regard some of my business students had for viewing business decisions from a Christian perspective. The business students that I taught were bright and energetic, and they do understand the importance of Christ in their lives. Unfortunately, some seemed too willing to confine Christ to nonbusiness issues. Many have adopted an attitude like that in the world of business: If you don't play according to secular rules, you are sure to lose. Like many others in business, these students do not look to their Christian faith for guidance when making ethical business decisions.

This point was driven home during one of my ethics classes. We were discussing the case of Napster. Napster was a very popular online service that allowed users to trade music from their own electronically stored collections. The company acted as a clearinghouse, keeping track of those who were logged on and the music that was available to trade. By logging on, a user could search for any song, identify who had it, and instantly download it. For example, let us say that you were interested in finding a recording of "That's Amore" by Dean Martin. You would log on to Napster and type in the name of the song. Napster would search the files of everyone else who was currently logged on and notify you of all those who had that particular song. You could then download the song from another person's computer. The novel thing about companies like Napster is that the company does not provide the music, only the connection between those who have the music and those who want it.

The unintended consequence of using Napster technology was that protecting intellectual property rights became more difficult. Intellectual property refers to such things as computer programs, books, songs, and paintings. Napster ran into conflict with copyright laws designed to protect the property rights of the creators of intellectual works. Artists and recording companies argued that by allowing users to trade copyrighted material without paying for it, Napster was providing people with the means to steal. When I asked my students if Napster encouraged stealing, the immediate response was a resounding "NO!" I then asked them to define *stealing*. They agreed upon the definition that stealing is "taking someone else's property without permission." To me, that sounds like what was happening with Napster. People were taking copyrighted material, owned by others, without paying for it. My students spent a great deal of time and energy trying to explain why using Napster was not equivalent to stealing. Their answers were less than convincing.

I believe that many of us are like my students when it comes to defining *sin*. We are good at identifying obvious sinful acts, such as stealing money from a cash register or shoplifting cosmetics. However, when it comes to the more subtle definitions that we know are implied by God's prohibition against stealing, we try to find a way out. Stealing is stealing whether it is done by a hardened criminal on the street or through a service we can access in the comfort of our own dorm room. A Christian approach to business ethics will force us to consider our faith and to apply what we know about God to our business lives. When we look at our business practices through the lens of God's Word, we not only gain a deeper appreciation for what God means in his Word, but we also become embarrassed as we grasp the implications of the way we have conducted our commercial affairs.

Having made my fair share of ethical blunders, I know how easy it is to follow in the footsteps of the world's business leaders. It was all too easy and tempting for me to block my Christian faith out of my work life. I believe that we need to convince Christians that trusting in Christ makes sound business sense. With this book my first goal is to reinforce our understanding that Christ goes to work with us every day. This means that a sin committed in the workplace is still a sin. On the other hand, his forgiveness and mercy are just as available at the office as they are in the church pew.

A second goal of this book is to highlight how economic forces shape the ethical decisions that we make. It is easy to paint businesses with the broad strokes of greed, ruthlessness, and insensitivity. When a firm shifts jobs to a foreign country, resulting in our friends or neighbors being laid off, we see an uncaring corporation. When a CEO gets what appears to be an astronomically large bonus or the corporation earns record profits, some of us see that as evidence of greed. And those views may be accurate. But to understand if what is going on in the world of business is ethical, we need to understand how Christian faith and economic forces influence business decisions.

This book assumes that the reader has a basic understanding of God's Word. The first part of the book will offer a view of the basic economic principles in the light of God's Word. Business decisions are made in the context of economic forces, and as we will see, God does say some things that relate to the structure of an economy. Christians not only consider the economic implications of their decisions but also how God will view those decisions. The second part of the book will apply economics and God's Word to current ethical problems facing businesses.

You won't find definitive answers to these problems within the pages of this book. No book is able to address the various complex questions that Christian businesspeople face. Each Christian will have to struggle with the application of God's Word to his or her individual business situation. But I hope that this book motivates businesspeople to start thinking about what it means to be a Christian who competes in the marketplace. Businesspeople need to remember that commerce also is a gift from God and that it falls within the scrutiny of his watchful eye. If we think about business in this context, we will gain an even deeper appreciation of what it means to be a Christian engaged in business. As Christians, we can view profits as the rewards that God bestows upon us for a job well done. How we make that money becomes the real issue. In chapter 1 we will emphasize that Christianity is a sound business strategy. Chapters 2 and 3 will explain how an economic system impacts business decisions. In chapters 4, 5, and 6, we will evaluate the capitalist economic system from a Christian perspective. Chapters 7 and 8 will link economic theory with Christian principles so that God-pleasing business decisions can be made. In chapter 9 we will take a quick detour and look at what Martin Luther had to say about economics and business. (It may surprise you.) Chapter 10 will focus on specific issues facing business leaders today.

ONE
CHRISTIANITY
as a business strategy

"The Christian ideal has not been tried and found wanting; it has been found difficult and left untried." —G. K. Chesterton

Master Lock, famous for locks that do not break even when pierced by a bullet, had been a part of the Milwaukee, Wisconsin, manufacturing scene since 1921. As recently as 1994, Master Lock controlled 70 percent of the nation's lock market.[1] At one time an economic anchor for the city, its plant provided 1,100 unionized manufacturing positions. The announcement that Fortune Brands, Master Lock's parent company, was moving the manufacturing to Mexico in order to cut costs sent shock waves through the city. Not only did Milwaukee lose a revered symbol of its once-powerful manufacturing muscle, but it also lost seven hundred jobs.[2] For the Christian, such a business decision would pose an ethical dilemma. What do we owe a community when we are engaged in business?

The goal of conducting business in a God-pleasing manner has challenged mankind since the fall into sin. Fourteen hundred years before Christ was born, Moses had to warn the Israelites about the dangers of engaging in unethical business practices. He wrote: "Do not have two differing weights in your bag—one heavy, one light. Do not have two differing measures in your house—one large, one small. You must have accurate and honest weights and measures, so that you may live long in the land the LORD your God is giving you. For the LORD your God detests anyone who does these things, anyone who deals dishonestly" (Deuteronomy 25:13-16). It is clear that

God's will for our lives applies also to our business lives. Sin is sin, even if it is committed in the pursuit of profit.

Approximately seven hundred years later, shady business practices were still plaguing God's chosen people. Amos again warned the Israelites about the dangers of engaging in unethical business practices. "Hear this, you who trample the needy and do away with the poor of the land, saying, 'When will the New Moon be over that we may sell grain, and the Sabbath be ended that we may market wheat?'—skimping the measure, boosting the price and cheating with dishonest scales, buying the poor with silver and the needy for a pair of sandals, selling even the sweepings with the wheat. The LORD has sworn by the Pride of Jacob: 'I will never forget anything they have done'" (8:4-7).

We may find it convenient to justify unethical behavior by saying, "Business is business." God clearly does not see it that way. God's will does not somehow change when we go to work in the morning.

Christ himself confronted a corrupt business world when he cast the money changers out of the temple. "On reaching Jerusalem, Jesus entered the temple area and began driving out those who were buying and selling there. He overturned the tables of the money changers and the benches of those selling doves, and would not allow anyone to carry merchandise through the temple courts. And as he taught them, he said, 'Is it not written: "My house will be called a house of prayer for all nations"? But you have made it "a den of robbers"'" (Mark 11:15-17). Almost 1,430 years after Moses, people still had not caught on that making money is not an acceptable substitute for God.

One danger of looking back through the pages of history is that it becomes so easy to judge those who have gone before us. An old saying in the game of Sheepshead states, "You always win the second time." After each hand is played and as the new cards are being dealt, players usually evaluate what went wrong or right with the last hand. It is not uncommon to hear someone say, "If I had just played a queen on that trick, things would have been different." How many of us would have set up shop in the temple court just before Christ came walking through? It is easy to deny that we would have been so foolish! We forget that if everyone were doing it and if we would have wanted to remain competitive, the temptation would have been just as great for us as it was for everyone else.

When all is said and done, we realize that we aren't much different than the merchants at the time of Christ, Amos, or Moses. Our scales may be more accurate and the government may enforce more laws, but the temptation to cheat is just as strong today as it was back then. The ethical dilemmas faced by today's businesspeople might be different, but that doesn't give us a license to ignore what God has to say. If anything, our ethical questions may be trickier than ever. Globalization means that businesses compete with other firms around the world. In America, the ethical standards may be different than they are overseas. How will Christians deal with the various customs they might encounter? What about the pressures to increase profit? Christians must balance the need to make money with an obligation to help the less fortunate, which might put a strain on profit. Finally, technological advances that allow companies to manipulate life also present complex ethical issues to Christians in business today. Should businesses be allowed to continue research using human embryos? As Christians, how do we become the "salt of the earth" and the "light of the world" in a capitalist environment?

We might apply that question to the situation at Master Lock.

The loss of a major employer can devastate a community in more ways than one. The most obvious effect is the loss of jobs that pay high wages. People employed in the service or retail industries typically do not earn as much as those employed in the manufacturing sector. In 1998, the average manufacturing job in Milwaukee paid approximately $42,464.[3] Working in retail, that same person would have earned $16,024.[4] Clearly the loss of a manufacturing firm deprives a community of at least one source of high-paying jobs.

3

Perhaps a less obvious effect is the uneven impact a company's departure has on various racial groups. Unemployment does not affect all racial groups evenly. This is particularly true in Milwaukee, because the city has a higher percentage of minorities than any other municipality in the state of Wisconsin.[5] According to government figures for the year 2000, unemployment among minorities was over four times higher than it was for white workers.[6] One explanation for the higher unemployment rate among minority groups is that they lack basic skills, work experience, and education.[7] Another problem might be that they lack the means to get to a job. Without a driver's license, car, or access to mass transit, jobs outside the immediate neighborhood are inaccessible.[8] Whatever the reason, the loss of jobs in the inner city, where a high proportion of the minority population lives, has an adverse effect on those groups.

A loss of jobs has a domino effect throughout the community. The economic consequences of unemployment can fray the social fabric of a city. If you drive through the area surrounding the Master Lock plant, you can still see the remnants of a once-bustling industrial neighborhood. The architecture of the single-family homes reflects the pride of a bygone generation. But today it is not uncommon for single-family homes near the Master Lock plant to sell for less than $50,000. Meanwhile, the median price of a single-family home in the city of Milwaukee was $87,175 in 2000.[9] And though commercial buildings along the business district are decaying because of abuse and abandonment, they still remind us of a time when economic prosperity was the norm and not the exception.

Economic statistics tell only part of the story. Too often in poor neighborhoods traditional families have been replaced by single-parent households. In one Milwaukee zip code, 91 percent of all children were born to unwed mothers.[10] Milwaukee has the sixth highest teen pregnancy rate in the nation.[11] Poverty rates in Milwaukee are considerably higher than in other parts of the state.[12] Among children, the poverty rate for Milwaukee County is almost twice the state average.[13] In some inner city neighborhoods, fewer than one in three children graduates from high school.[14]

Crime is another major social problem plaguing Milwaukee. Inner city neighborhoods, like the one that surrounds the Master Lock plant, have some of the highest rates of murder, arson, rape, and theft in the city.[15] These problems were not created solely by poor economic conditions, nor will they be solved by an improving economy. However, one wonders how people can begin to improve their lot in life if they do not possess minimal economic resources.

Master Lock's decision to transfer jobs to Mexico was not the cause of the socioeconomic woes confronting the city of Milwaukee. Master Lock was not the first company to move out of the city. Nor will it be the last. The point of this analysis is that because manufacturing jobs are so important for a city and a local neighborhood, we must not forget that economic decisions have social ramifications. As businesspeople, our goal is to make a profit. As Christians, our goal is to serve. The apostle Paul reminds us in Galatians 5:13 that we are to "serve one another in love." Does the elimination of jobs in a community that has supported the company for 80 years fulfill the spirit of Paul's words? How we make the decisions that will impact a countless number of people beyond our employees is not an insignificant issue.

For Master Lock, moving jobs to Mexico made economic sense. Between 1994 and 1997, Master Lock's market share dwindled from 70 percent to 40 percent.[16] Large retailers like Wal-Mart and Target had begun to sell cheap imported locks from China. American consumers were simply not willing to pay for high-priced locks when quality alternatives were available for substantially lower prices. If Master Lock was going to compete with cheap imports, it had to cut costs.

In business, one of the largest controllable expenses is labor. In an effort to reduce labor costs, Fortune Brands decided to move Master Lock's manufacturing operation from its Milwaukee facility to its plant in Nogales, Mexico. As a result, the Milwaukee workforce was reduced from 1,160 to 350 people. At the same time, the number of Master Lock employees in Mexico increased from two hundred people to eight hundred. The wage differential between the Mexico and Milwaukee plants saved Fortune Brands $16 million annually.[17]

A strong case can be made for moving the jobs from Milwaukee to Mexico. No company can stay in business if it is operating at a substantial cost disadvantage. By making the move, Master Lock is now more price competitive, allowing Fortune Brands to hire five hundred additional workers at its other facilities in the United States.[18] The move certainly seems to have made economic sense. Of course, executives of large corporations seldom have ties to the local community where their factories are located. Because they do not live in those communities, closing plants and laying off people have no direct impact on them. They do not personally experience the ramifications of their decisions.

A Christian, however, recognizes that closing a plant is not simply a question of economics. The question must be viewed in tandem with the question of whether the economic concerns justify terminating a labor relationship. Nowhere in the Bible will the Christian find a direct answer to this question. This adds to the frustration some of us feel when confronted with difficult choices. Indeed, instead of finding a Bible passage with a one-size-fits-all answer, the Christian will need to focus on what being a member of Christ's kingdom really means. We know that the Son of God died for our sins so that we might have eternal life. The eternal freedom that is ours in Christ establishes the ethical context for our decisions. Christians enjoy a personal relationship with God himself. As such, everything we do and think flows from a humble spirit that reveres God for the undeserved love he has shown us. This recognition of God's undeserved love will set the tone for the way we live in our relationships with others—and also our business relationships.

In order to reflect God's love for us in Christ through our business relationships, we need to have a firm grasp not only of Christian doctrine, but also of economic principles.

And that's not just the concern of businesspeople. As consumers and laborers, we too are influenced by economic forces. We love lower prices at the store but demand higher wages. We often view decisions to move production to another location or to lay off workers as proof that management is greedy. The fact that business has to be competitive in order to pay our wages we don't see as our problem. My hope for all of us nonbusinesspersons is the same as my hope for our brothers and sisters who are in business. How we conduct ourselves in the marketplace may or may not reflect God's glory. Like businesspeople, we too need to think about the economic influences that shape the way we live our lives as Christians.

TWO

A CHRISTIAN
view of economics

"If all economists were laid end to end, they would not reach a conclusion." —*George Bernard Shaw*

If Wisconsin is America's Dairyland, where have all the farms gone? In 1950, 174,000 farms were operating in Wisconsin. By 2000, that number had dwindled to 77,000.[1] If you look carefully as you drive through Wisconsin, you can see where the farms have gone. It is relatively easy to find old farmhouses in Milwaukee and its suburbs, reminding us how much this metropolitan area has grown. It is even easier to find visual remnants of old farmsteads in rural Wisconsin. Dilapidated barns, abandoned houses, and rusted machinery still stand as testimonies to the attempts of some intrepid homesteaders to make a living off the land.

To answer the question, farms are being converted to other uses. Subdivisions are replacing cornfields and pastures as lush farmlands are transformed into bedroom communities.

Perhaps the real question is not Where have all the farms gone? but, Why have so many small farms disappeared? And the question doesn't have to be limited to agriculture. Drive through just about any small town's business district, and the question becomes, Where have the small businesses gone? Like the abandoned farm buildings that dot the countryside, empty buildings on Main Street remind us that something in the economy has changed. My dad made an interesting observation to this point. In 1950, with a population of only 2,600 people, Neillsville, Wisconsin, had 12 grocery stores. Today the population of Neillsville is still approximately 2,600 people, but now there are only two grocery stores. My dad muses over the reasons why this is so. And an academic answer does not satisfy him.

The conversion of a farm into a subdivision or a small grocery store into a supermarket is more than just an economic issue. For Christians, economic activity raises some fundamental ethical issues that need to be examined. One has to do with stewardship. For example, how do Christians who participate in a market economy view competition? Is moving a factory to Mexico, as in the case of Master Lock, an example of personal greed, an attempt to improve efficiency, or the result of market forces over which management had no control? The same question applies when productive farmland is converted to alternative uses. I have often heard people describe developers as being greedy or large firms like Wal-Mart as being detrimental to the community because they destroy small businesses. If we, consumers, demand the products that the developer or Wal-Mart offers, whose motives need to be examined?

A second fundamental ethical issue facing Christians competing in a market economy is the question of how to deal with the human consequences of competition. A free market can be a ruthless arena that takes no prisoners. As we will soon see, the emphasis on economic efficiency will yield many positive results in terms of material wealth. On the flip side, economic efficiency may result in lower wages and/or fewer benefits, the termination of older employees, or the shuttering of a business. It is common to hear people suggest that profitable companies are getting rich at the expense of poorly paid employees. We would like these companies to share the wealth. When they don't do it according to our expectations, we accuse them of exploiting labor or the community. But how do Christian managers balance the need to make a profit with the responsibility to look out for the less fortunate among us? The stewardship issue and the question of how to deal with the human consequences of competition will be dealt with in subsequent chapters. In this chapter, I want to establish the fact that economic forces can shape our attitudes toward others and the government.

Economics has been described as the study of scarcity. Living as we do in a sinful world, scarcity is a fact of life. One of my daughter's favorite expressions is "There is always more in the store." There may be more in the store, but that does precious little good if you do not have enough money to make a purchase. Because of limited resources, we cannot fully satisfy our material wants and needs. Even though Ted Turner, the charismatic founder of CNN, may be able to give millions to the United Nations and still have enough to add thousands of acres to his New Mexico ranch, his divorce from Jane Fonda underscores the fact that money does not buy everything. For most of us, time, talent, and money are in short supply. Not only does my wallet always seem empty, but it seems that there is never enough time in a day to finish my list of projects. And though I would like to play basketball with my son, a lack of talent forced me to abandon that activity years ago.

Scarcity forces each of us to make choices. How can we satisfy our material needs with the resources that are available? The choices that we make depend on whether we are buying or selling. As consumers, we want to buy the most we can for the lowest possible cost. Because I am cheap, my rule of thumb is to go for quantity over quality. Though it drives my friends crazy, I find it difficult to change. Sellers prefer to sell at the highest price possible.

It is this interaction between buyers and sellers that determines what products and services are bought and sold in the market, and at what price. When consumers want more of a product than is being supplied, the price goes up. Conversely, when suppliers offer more than is demanded, prices drop.

The power of consumer choice cannot be underestimated. Firms will not spend limited resources producing a product the consumer does not want. To do so would result in financial loss. The Ford Motor Company learned this lesson the hard way between 1957 and 1960. After investing approximately $250 million on research and production, the people at Ford had great expectations for their new showcase model, the Edsel. Unfortunately, consumers were not nearly as excited. After three years of disappointing sales, the line was dropped—a testament to the power of consumer choice.

Coca-Cola learned a similar lesson in 1985. On April 23, Coca-Cola replaced its original version of Coke with "New Coke." New Coke was cheaper to make, and market research indicated that consumers preferred it to the original formula. However, contrary to the predictions of marketing professionals, consumers were so outraged that on July 11, 1985, Coca-Cola announced it was switching back to its old formula.[2] It does not matter how good the company thinks a product is—if the consumer does not buy it, the investment is a waste. Henry Ford summed it up nicely when he said: "It is not the employer who pays the wages—he only handles the money. It is the product that pays the wages."

An important point to remember is that self-interest is the engine that drives our choices. The government does not order the local Dodge dealership to sell sport-utility vehicles (SUVs). The local Dodge dealer sells SUVs because it can make a profit. Maximizing profit is in the self-interest of every business. Likewise, no bureaucratic agency orders consumers to shop at Wal-Mart. Consumers shop there because it is in their self-interest to get as many products as needed for the lowest possible price. The same principle can be applied to our jobs. We work where we do because our jobs allow us to achieve some desired benefit. When our jobs no longer deliver these benefits, most of us will look for other work.

I want to make a very important point about self-interest. We should not equate self-interest with greed. They are not the same thing. In economics, self-interest can be a positive motivating force. Self-interest implies that we look toward the future to understand the consequences of our actions—not only for ourselves but for our loved ones and neighbors. We take into account how much our choices might cost ourselves and others. Greed ignores the long-term implications of a decision and the impact that the decision has on others. Greed distorts economic decision-making because it fails to adequately account for all the costs implicit in any given choice.

When scarcity, choice, and self-interest intersect in the marketplace, the result is competition among different buyers, different sellers, and buyers and sellers. Did you ever wonder why there are more than 26 different shades of red lipstick at Walgreens? Any woman or anyone in a close relationship with a woman knows why. The economic answer is that to offer a wider variety of products is one way for businesses to attract new customers. Competition also forces businesses to continually improve their existing product line or offer new products. Think about how much faster, more powerful, and less expensive personal computers are today compared to ten years ago. Other examples of how competition encourages the production of newer and better products include DVD players that have replaced VCRs, cell phones that have replaced hard-wired home phones, and minivans that have replaced the full-sized station wagon with wood side-paneling. Competition between buyers and sellers drives product improvement, innovation, and selection. It also helps lower prices.

Markets, through competition, establish prices that ultimately dictate what will be bought and sold and who will make the purchase. For example, in 1998 Mark McGwire of the Saint Louis Cardinals was in a home-run derby with Sammy Sosa of the Chicago Cubs. At stake was the single season home-run record previously set in 1961 by Roger Maris of the New York Yankees. McGwire and Sosa were tied for the lead when McGwire's Cardinals came to Milwaukee County Stadium for the Brewer's final home stand of the season. Having received four free tickets, my family and I went to the game. McGwire hit a towering shot in the first inning to notch his 65th home run of the season. A follow-up blast to the centerfield wall in the fifth inning was ruled a ground rule double because of fan interference. My wife did not care, my kids were bored, but I thought that McGwire had been robbed. In any event, with the Brewers down by what appeared to be an insurmountable lead, we left the park. On our way out, a young entrepreneur approached me to buy my ticket stubs. I sold him four ticket stubs for $10 and went home quite pleased with myself.

The moral to this story is not how shrewd my negotiating skills are (They are not!), but how supply and demand influence price. The only way I can explain the sale that day is that the young entrepreneur thought the ticket stubs for that game were going to appreciate in value. His demand for ticket stubs was greater than my desire to keep them, so, at $2.50 apiece, I supplied four ticket stubs. Let us now assume that one of the home runs hit by McGwire that day at County Stadium became the hit that clinched his home-run title and record. Baseball enthusiasts would be willing to pay far more than $2.50 for one of those ticket stubs. Since the number of tickets would be limited, the only way to increase the available supply would be to increase the purchase price. As the price offered for a ticket stub increases, more people would be willing to sell their ticket stubs. At some point, collectors will pay no more for a ticket and suppliers will sell for no less. This then becomes the market price. Whether we are talking about ticket stubs or unleaded gasoline, the pricing mechanism ultimately governs production and consumption.

Though consumers welcome competition because it often results in more choices and lower prices, suppliers often react differently. Competition can turn business dealings into brutal combat that takes no prisoners. An example of a market that has an ample number of competitors would be dairy farming. Each farmer sells the milk at the current market price. A problem with dairy farming is that there is not much difference between the milk produced on one farm and the milk produced on a farm in another state. Kemps' 2-percent milk looks and tastes pretty much like Golden Guernsey's 2-percent milk. Though there are many farmers, they are not in positions to dictate the price of their milk. If one farmer refuses to sell the milk, the resulting shortage will be a mere drop in the bucket. Because there are so many other farmers, his action will have very little impact on the market price. In 1967 the National Farmers Organization (NFO) encouraged its members to dump their milk instead of sell it because the price being paid to producers was too low. Organizers hoped that this dumping action might drive the price of milk higher. The flaw in the plan was that the NFO did not have enough members to influence the price. Because the amount of milk they dumped was small compared to the overall supply, the only thing the NFO accomplished was depriving its members of their paychecks.[3]

Farmers are not the only ones constrained by market forces. Companies like United Air Lines, Inc. and Kmart are two of the most recent examples of companies that are suffering from the effects of intense competition. Both companies are trying to sell products and services that are readily available elsewhere. The traveling public does not need United. People can buy cheaper seats to desirable destinations from discount airlines. Kmart offers the same products as Wal-Mart, Target, and a host of other retailers. Unfortunately for Kmart, the other chains offer these products either more cheaply, at better locations, or in more shopper-friendly environments. If Kmart and United are unable to attract more buyers for their services, they will cease to exist.

To survive in business, companies must continually strive to provide the goods and services consumers want—at prices that they will pay.

Providing new or improved products are two ways to satisfy consumers. A third way is to sell products at lower prices. The key to lowering prices lies in productivity. By producing more goods and services without increasing costs, the seller should be able to increase profits.

Let's say that Ford Motor Company has $1 million to spend on car production. If Ford used 1920s technology and production methods, let us assume that it would cost $10,000 to manufacture one car. Ford would produce, and society would get, one hundred cars. By adopting computer technology, advanced production techniques, and modern management practices, let us now assume that Ford can produce the same car for $5,000. Given these assumptions, society would now get two hundred cars and Ford would get additional revenue. All else being equal, improved production methods would allow Ford to manufacture more cars with the same amount of resources.

Competition, scarcity, choice, and self-interest all contribute to economic efficiency. We participate in the market so that we can satisfy our individual material needs. The collective choices that we make dictate the selections of products and services that stores will offer. Through competition, the market forces businesses to provide the goods and services consumers demand—at the lowest possible prices. The end result is that we are better off materially. Just look around your house at your material possessions. Note the variety of products that you own. We all have been incredibly blessed.

But competition can have dramatic effects on the marketplace. At the beginning of this chapter, I asked why so many farms have disappeared from the landscape. Economic theory gives us the answer. Productivity gains have made American agriculture incredibly efficient. The labor required to produce one hundred bushels of corn has fallen from 106 hours in 1910 to 7 hours today. In three minutes, a modern dairy farmer can get the same amount of milk that it took a WWI-era farmer one hour to produce.[4] The development of more powerful tractors, larger implements, new chemicals, improved fertilizers, genetically enhanced seeds, a more efficient transportation system, and rural electrification have made it possible for fewer farmers to raise more crops per acre than at any time in the history of the United States. The fact is that this country needs fewer farmers to raise the food that we consume.

My father has a hard time accepting the fact that economic efficiency has resulted in the existence of fewer farms. For my father, the disappearance of small family farms, neighborhood grocery stores, feed mills, and auto dealerships are a sad commentary on our society. He was further disappointed by the news that General Motors (GM) was eliminating the Oldsmobile after one hundred years of production. (Some of us, for noneconomic reasons, believe that GM is actually doing society a favor by eliminating the Oldsmobile!) I have tried using economic theory to explain to him that society no longer needs as many feed mills, grocery stores, or automobile brands when a few larger companies can provide the same products and services for less money, but my father still thinks we are losing something meaningful.

While economists would quickly dismiss my father's rationale, he may have a point. At the very least, we Christians need to think about what he has to say. I believe that my father is disturbed by the loss of "community" that he once knew. He loves to tell about all the small farms that dotted the countryside around our home. With less than one hundred acres, these farms provided a living for entire families. My father will also list all the grocery stores, bars, feed mills, implement dealers, and car dealerships that lined the streets of my hometown. Most of them are gone now. But at one time, each of these businesses also provided a livelihood for a family. Today it's nearly impossible to earn a living on a farm with less than two hundred acres. And the corner grocery store and the local hardware store have been replaced by a one-hundred-thousand-square-foot behemoth like the Wal-Mart Supercenter.

The ethical implication of economic efficiency is that while we have more products and services than ever before, our attitude toward other people may have been sacrificed. Christ reminds us that he came to earth to serve, not to be served—and that we should follow his example. The Scriptures urge us to help those in need. Economic efficiency and progress aside, Christians should still care for one another. When I see how impersonal business has become, I begin to appreciate what my father means. No matter how many personalized solicitations I get from Visa, I do not believe that the company really cares about me as an individual.

The last store I managed was in a town that was soon to get a Wal-Mart. Shortly after Wal-Mart began hiring employees for its store, my district manager called to tell me that our company was closing my store. He further informed me that I could take a transfer to a new store in Missouri or take a demotion with a corresponding pay cut. The call came at 3:00 P.M. My boss gave me until 7:00 P.M. that same night to make a decision.

More important and more disturbing than my predicament was the way in which he wanted me to treat my employees. I was to say nothing to my employees about the impending closure of the store—and this despite the fact that Wal-Mart was in the process of hiring new employees. It was my company's opinion that if the community found out prematurely about the closure, employees would quit, leaving the store difficult to manage during the liquidation. As a result, sales would be needlessly lost. But the community afforded very few opportunities for permanent, year-round, full-time work. Failure to inform my employees of the impending layoffs might have meant that some would not have had the opportunity to apply for the full-time positions at Wal-Mart.

I think about how easy it would have been to say nothing to my employees, take the transfer to Missouri, and continue moving up the corporate ladder. I had no commitment to that town. It was like all the other towns I had lived in while pursuing my career. The people were nice, but I did not know them that well. And I had always known that, at some point, I would be moving on. Secure in the knowledge that I would be getting a pay raise and a new opportunity, I could have said nothing to them. I could have easily ignored their losses because I never again would have had to look them in the eyes as we met on the sidewalk.

Countless people in America have experienced my dilemma. Economists can tell us that, in the end, we are better off when a more efficient firm like Wal-Mart replaces less-efficient competition. Using economic theory, we can probably even prove it. What is harder to explain is the loss that my father feels. There is nothing in economic theory to account for the loss of human relationships. In the relentless pursuit of economic efficiency, the sense of community, of concern for neighbors, and of compassion for those in need has been trampled along the way.

Pursuing business success at the expense of human relationships is not an acceptable practice for Christians. Even though it meant dying a gruesome death on the cross, Christ did not put his self-interest ahead of ours. How can we take the command to look to the cross for guidance seriously if we turn our backs on those in need? As a Christian manager, failing to tell my employees that they were about to lose their jobs would have been wrong. We need to remember that our Lord died to save people, not to ensure economic efficiency. To make efficiency our priority is to make a mockery of what we believe and confess.

Our economic system not only influences the way we view our relations with others, but it also shapes our view of government. An economic system that relies on supply and demand as a pricing mechanism theoretically limits the role government needs to play in the economy. A properly functioning market will self-adjust, reflecting the current choices of consumers. Sellers will produce only what can be sold. The government ends up being like a referee in a boxing match. Its role is to make sure that everyone plays by the rules—albeit a very limited number of rules. Critics insist that any role the government plays is too large a role. They contend that when the government gets involved, the interference distorts the market and results in economic waste and inefficiency.

Critics of government have a point, but they shouldn't overplay their hand. The recent utility deregulation in California is an example. On March 31, 1998, California began to implement a partial deregulation of the electric utility industry. The plan "created a system that dispersed power plant ownership, put control of the electricity superhighway in the hands of a disinterested third party and created an open auction where power can be purchased at the lowest price."[5] The goal was to reduce the cost of electricity by opening up the market to competition. Supporters of deregulation believed that if consumers could pick their supplier, as they were able to with long-distance telephone service, costs would drop as producers would compete to provide electricity reliably and cheaply.

By late 2000 it was clear that deregulation was not working. While the state's largest utility, Pacific Gas and Electric, filed for bankruptcy protection, rolling blackouts left customers without lights. The peak cost of a megawatt of electricity in December 2000 was $1500, significantly higher than the $30 per megawatt that customers had paid in April of 1998.[6] The cause for the debacle has been blamed on everything from inadequate supplies and increased demand to a poorly crafted deregulation plan.[7] Whatever the cause, deregulation "California style" fell short of its lofty goal.

Contrary to the rhetoric of free-market proponents, a lack of government regulation may have contributed to waste and inefficiency. North Carolina's utility, Duke Energy, was accused of "systematically engaging in a price-fixing conspiracy through unlawful trading practices to manipulate the state's electricity market."[8] The company was later accused of making a deal with the state. It agreed to stop charging a premium for electricity and to accept less than the $20 billion it originally claimed it was owed if the state agreed to stop investigating the company's pricing policies, curtailed litigation, and ceased blaming the current energy crisis on deregulation.[9] Federal regulators have already ordered Duke Energy to refund $20 million in overcharges.[10]

Duke Energy is not the only utility accused of profiting unfairly from the California energy crisis. After selling $2.65 billion worth of electricity to California, a British Columbia utility gave rebates to its customers from excess profits. A company spokesman denied that the profits were a result of the California sales.[11] Meanwhile, a local consumer group accused power producers of intentionally withholding power to artificially inflate the price of electricity. It claimed that "as much as 13,000 [megawatts] of capacity was off-line in January for undisclosed reasons. According to the *Wall Street Journal*, on August 2000, 461 percent more capacity was off-line than a year earlier."[12] While no one has yet proven the existence of an intentional plot to defraud electric utility customers, the circumstantial evidence is growing. As one activist noted, "Regardless of whether one suspects that power producers are intentionally taking capacity off-line to hike prices, these statistics illustrate that under deregulation, the public has little control over pricing and reliability."[13]

The utility deregulation controversy in California provides a suitable backdrop for Christians to reevaluate their behavior in the marketplace and their view of government regulation. Some critics of government contend that if the market were left to operate on its own, there would be no need for government regulation. Proponents of government regulation point out that market inefficiencies result in inequities that need to be corrected. Given the sinful world in which we live, Christians should not automatically view government involvement in the economy as wrong. The government is an institution ordained by God. If, through rules and regulations, it curbs sin and protects the interests of its people, who are we to dismiss its role?

With or without government regulation, the Christian conducts business according to a different set of goals than that of the non-Christian. Reaching a higher profit margin on electricity sales because the market has pushed up prices relative to cost is not wrong. Creating or contributing to a crisis for personal gain is another story. The Christian needs to make sure that the allure of profit does not damage his or her relationship with God. By focusing on profit as the overriding goal, we are in danger of violating the First Commandment's admonition to have no other gods. Our primary goal on this earth is to love, trust, and obey God. We have God's promise that he will provide whatever we need. Thinking that we must earn all we can so that we will be comfortable in our golden years flies in the face of this promise.

THREE

EQUITY, EFFICIENCY, and economics— a moral connection

> "No amount of ability is of the slightest avail without honor." —*Andrew Carnegie*

Gehl Company, a manufacturer of construction and farm equipment, has been a part of the West Bend, Wisconsin, economy since 1859. Farm equipment accounts for half of Gehl's sales but only a very small percentage of profits.[1] Over the years, various investors have held differing opinions about the priorities of the company. In the past, some investors believed that the farm equipment division should be sold because it was depressing the company's stock price. When a stock price remains low relative to the purchase price, shareholders earn less on their investments than if they would have invested in some other instrument of equal risk. Other investors believed that because the firm was too small to compete in the market, it should be sold to a larger firm.[2]

Bill Gehl sold neither the farm division nor the company. Was this the right decision? Employees of Gehl and residents of West Bend are probably happy with Mr. Gehl's decision. Gehl employs four hundred people at its production facility and corporate headquarters in West Bend.[3] Selling the company or shuttering the production facility would almost certainly have meant a loss of jobs. The residents probably saw the company as part of the foundation of the community. The shareholders probably saw it differently. An important responsibility of management is to maximize shareholder value. If the company is underperforming in the market, as alleged, shareholders, who are the legal owners of the company, are being cheated out of the full return on their investments.

When a company underperforms in the market, a number of factors can be blamed. Two factors that were pertinent to the situation at Gehl focus on potential and management. The people fighting to take control of the company believed that Gehl was too small to compete with larger firms, like Caterpillar. If the company were not sold, they reasoned, it would eventually lose market share and possibly end up in bankruptcy. A second argument had to do with mismanagement. Not only can weak management hurt a company financially, but the perceived weakness can cause investors to shun the stock, which drives down the value of the business even more. By trying to get rid of Gehl's weak management, investors were hoping to revitalize the company.

It would be easy to paint the new investors as greedy takeover artists who were fixated on short-term profits. That very well may have been true. However, in order to use economic resources as efficiently as possible, perhaps the company should have been sold. Preserving an entrenched management style that fails to generate an acceptable rate of return is not good stewardship. Yet destroying the jobs of hundreds of employees for the sake of a quick dollar on Wall Street also seems to fall short of the good-stewardship standard. Very often in business the legitimate goals and interests of owners and labor collide. Before we can assess who is right or wrong, we must first appreciate how the economy shapes business decisions.

The nations of the world choose between two basic economic systems: capitalism and socialism. God does not mandate a particular system. The hallmarks of capitalism, or a free market, are private property, individual choice, competition, and limited government control. A socialist system emphasizes government planning, income redistribution from the wealthy to the less fortunate, and government ownership of the resources needed for production. These resources include natural resources, productive capital (factories, computers, tools, etc.), labor, and entrepreneurship. Winston Churchill described the difference between the two systems in this way: "The vice of capitalism is that it stands for the unequal sharing of blessings; whereas the virtue of socialism is that it stands for the equal sharing of misery."[4] As much as we may prefer capitalism, we need to ask whether this economic system is compatible with our Christian faith. That is the focus of chapter 4.

One of the keys of the capitalistic system is the right of private citizens to own property. Property rights give the owner the privilege of using the resource as he or she sees fit. The idea is that ownership will encourage investment, innovation, and risk taking with the promise of increased returns. Exxon, Toyota, and GM announced on January 1, 2001, that they had formed an alliance to develop an environmentally friendly fuel cell.[5] The hope is that the new technology will replace the internal combustion engine. It is hard to imagine that these companies would invest in such a venture if they would not be allowed to reap the benefits.

In a socialist economic system, the fairness of markets is often an issue. A socialist has less confidence in the pricing mechanism than a capitalist does. While proponents of a free-market system believe that the forces of supply and demand establish prices, critics see the underhanded influence of business at play. For example, in the summer of 2000, gasoline prices in the Midwest increased dramatically to over $2 a gallon. Many people believed that the oil companies were behind the price increase. However, after a nine-month investigation, the Federal Trade Commission concluded that while some firms did try to maximize their profits, "the principle causes of the price spike were largely beyond the immediate control of industry participants."[6] In a socialist economic system, the government would have been more willing to use regulatory controls to lessen the impact or to prevent the price increase from occurring.

The socialists' distrust of the pricing mechanism can be traced to their suspicion of the marketplace itself. As we have seen, in a capitalist economy, firms and individuals compete in the marketplace. This competition dictates price. Socialism tends to view markets as being the unwitting tools of big business. These businesses manipulate consumer preferences through advertising and pricing policies. Whether we agree with the socialists' position or not, the Midwest gasoline shortage in 2000 and the California energy crisis of 2001 show that we cannot dismiss their views out of hand. And the ethics surrounding advertising are worth a closer look.

Socialists tend to view private-property ownership as the source of political power. As such, those who have amassed enormous amounts of private property have an unfair political advantage over the less fortunate. Therefore, socialists are more willing to use government sanctions than their capitalist counterparts. Later we will address the proper role of government in the marketplace and how that role influences a Christian businessperson's decisions.

Economic systems are neither inherently good nor bad. They simply reflect different views of the market. Regardless of the type, all economic systems have to answer three fundamental questions: What goods and services will be produced? How will the goods and services be produced? For whom will the goods and services be produced?

The first question—What goods and services will be produced?—acknowledges that society will be unable to produce everything it desires. In the United States, consumer choice dictates which private products will be produced. Private products are those items whose uses are limited to those who purchase them. For example, I may really want to own a new Dodge Intrepid. But unless I go to a dealership and purchase one, it doesn't matter how many DaimlerChrysler produces; I will be out of luck—unless I have a really generous neighbor who loves to purchase cars for people. Since I don't, I won't reap the benefits of owning the car unless I decide to spend the money.

Not all goods are "private." Roads, schools, military defense, and parks are examples of what economists call public goods. The benefits of these products and services are not limited only to those who purchase them. Defense spending is an example. Some people object to military spending for nuclear weapons. They may even withhold a portion of their taxes in protest. This doesn't mean that their share of national defense is reduced, however. If attacked, the military will defend supporters and opponents of military policy equally. Another example is a local city park that does not charge admission. All citizens have equal access to the park, but only city taxpayers pay for its upkeep. Choices about public goods are determined by elections and reflected in government budgets.

The question of how the goods and services will be produced focuses on production methods. In a socialist economy, food is produced on collective farms owned by the state. Food was produced this way in the former Soviet Union, as well as in China even today. Most American farmers own their own land and choose the production methods that suit their goals. Large corporate farms invest heavily in new technology and the latest equipment to increase yields. The Amish choose to use more antiquated methods. A drive through an area like Greenwood, Wisconsin—home to a large concentration of Amish farmers—is a study in agricultural contrast. Shunning gasoline engines and other modern conveniences, the Amish still use horses to till the land. Meanwhile, their non-Amish neighbors may have the latest John Deere tractor. It is all about choices.

The final consideration of either economic system is the question of who will receive the goods and services that are produced. In a capitalist, or market, system, only those who are willing and able to pay for a product will enjoy the benefits of that purchase. In a socialist system, the government will make that choice. Medical care is an example. In the United States, access to medical care depends upon one's ability to pay. Those without insurance, cash resources, or the qualifications for government programs simply do not have access to the most advanced medical system in the world. In the United States, this means that one in five people are excluded. Across the border in Canada, society has determined that everyone should be entitled to affordable medical care. The Canadian government, not the market, dictates who has access to medical care.

To understand the differences between the two economic systems and to see how each gives different answers to the three fundamental questions outlined earlier, let us examine the collapse of Soviet communism in 1989. With the collapse, socialism seemed to be discredited as a viable economic system. Many former Soviet states replaced their totalitarian regimes and government-controlled economies with democracies linked to free markets. Despite the renewed popularity of capitalism, a closer review of the assumptions for the underpinning of the economic system should give Christians pause. The same is true of a socialist economic system. Either system can divert our attention from our Lord and Savior.

A socialist economic system, with its reliance on government intervention in the market, is supposed to correct the inevitable inequities that plague capitalist economies. The health care system in the United States is an example. To many it seems grossly unfair that people can be denied health care because they are unable to pay. Countries with a socialist economic system have made health care a fundamental human right. In those countries, the government is responsible for ensuring that all people have access to the health care system.

Social welfare policies such as health care, unemployment insurance, retirement pensions, job security, and education traditionally have been used as political shorthand to differentiate between capitalist and socialist economic systems. This was very apparent during the Cold War between the United States and the former Soviet Union. Soviet leaders would highlight the advantages of socialism by pointing to the fact that Soviet citizens did not suffer from unemployment, homelessness, poverty, or lack of education. The Soviet government made sure that all citizens were provided these basic necessities. Of course, in the capitalist United States, certain classes of people were unemployed, homeless, or without access to schools and health care facilities. Critics of capitalism saw the system practiced in the United States as being unfair.

However, by the time Mikhail Gorbachev became General Secretary of the Soviet Union in 1985, his country was close to economic collapse. One reason was low labor productivity. Labor productivity is partially determined by the quality of the employee. By the early 1980s, alcoholism had become a national epidemic that reduced the life expectancy of males to 62 years.[7] If employees are sick, hungover, or in otherwise poor health, their productivity will likely drop.

Quality control also contributed to the economic woes facing the Soviet Union. Making something is a waste of time, effort, and resources if it cannot be used. Shoddy products that cannot be sold result in financial loss to the company. If the company does not make money, employees cannot be paid. One 1987 Soviet survey found that of 59 Moscow firms, only 20 percent produced acceptable outputs.[8] By the early 1990s, labor productivity and gross domestic product (GDP)[9] were both declining while inflation was increasing.[10] The economy was producing fewer goods, which were becoming more expensive, leaving ordinary Soviet citizens worse off financially.

While economists measure economic well-being in terms of GDP, labor productivity, and inflation, the rest of us look at our standard of living. By 1990 things were very bleak for the Russian population. One in four Russians, according to estimates, were living in poverty. Shortages of food and other consumer goods became acute. According to the Ministry of Internal Affairs, 98 percent of 1,100 selected consumer goods were not regularly available in state retail outlets. And the consumption of meat and dairy products by the poorest of Russians had declined by 30 percent since 1970.[11]

Health and housing conditions were just as bad. Approximately one-third of the population was existing in a "living space of less than nine square meters per person."[12] In the United States today, this figure is closer to 80 square meters.[13] Ninety percent of all school children suffered vitamin

27

deficiencies. "Half of Soviet schools had no central heating, running water, or indoor toilets."[14] Medicines simply weren't available, and one in six hospital beds were located in facilities that had no hot water. One medical expert complained that his facility had not received a Soviet-built ultrasound machine in 30 years.[15] By any measure, life in the Soviet Union had become a challenge.

Clearly some of the blame for the substandard living conditions in the former Soviet Union can be attributed to the failure of a centrally planned economy. A 1997 study of the USSR Academy of Sciences by the Institute for the World Economy and International Relations concluded, "The totalitarian, command, non-market economy could not be competitive with a developed market economy and its failure was in accordance with the historical law of 'survival of the fittest.'"[16] As early as 1986, some Soviet officials were exploring the possibility of giving employees incentives and bonuses to improve productivity.[17] Even Mikhail Gorbachev recognized the problems created by a socialist economy when he stated, "We had to change life radically, break away from the past malpractice."[18] But when Gorbachev tried to revitalize the economy through perestroika ("economic restructuring") and glasnost ("openness"), the entire system collapsed like a house of cards.

The collapse of socialism in the Soviet Union can be seen as a failure of the market to provide the goods and services consumers demanded at the lowest possible prices. This happened because the government did not respond to market signals. Soviet bureaucrats determined what would be produced, not a market that represented consumer demand. As a result, so many resources were spent producing industrial goods and military equipment that there were very few left for the production of consumer goods. Think of what life would be like in the United States if we did not have the wide variety of options for food, clothing, cars, and entertainment that we currently enjoy. I have 50 channels on my television, and I still am not happy. Many people around the world would love to have a television, period.

From the Christian perspective, the lack of competition is a serious deficiency of the socialist economic system. When resources are wasted by employees who have poor work ethics, the producers will never achieve low production costs. Producing low-quality goods and services, or those that are not wanted, is clearly a waste of time, talent, and treasure. God expects us to work so that we can support our families and ourselves. Even before sin entered the world, Adam was at work in the Garden of Eden. Our Lord also wants us to be good stewards of his creation. Throughout the Bible, God makes it clear that the earth and all that is in it belong to him. We are to use all things in such ways that he is glorified. It is hard to imagine that producing substandard products could glorify God's name.

A poor work ethic and wasted resources do not reflect the standard God has set for us. Socialism can encourage a poor work ethic by making people dependent on the government for all of their needs. Soviet employees had very little incentive to work hard, because the government provided for most of their material needs. And harder work would not have resulted in the ability to buy a better car, bigger house, or another television, because these products were not available. The lack of incentives contributed to their wastefulness and lack of productivity. We need to understand that efforts to achieve social equity that reduce personal responsibility and initiative can lead to waste.

Socialism also violates principles of good stewardship by encouraging waste. In the Soviet Union, the government owned most of the property. The managers of Soviet industries had no incentive to use limited resources wisely and efficiently. Without competition, these companies lacked incentives to improve quality, selection, and service. By guaranteeing a market for the products, the Soviet government eliminated any fear of bankruptcy. Without ownership interest, managers and employees lacked incentive to care, even to work. Problems such as alcohol abuse and corruption slowly rotted the economy from within, resulting in the enormous waste of resources.

I do not want to suggest that waste and corruption are present only in socialist economies. Our capitalist economy has seen plenty of both. Investors lost millions of dollars when the dot-com bubble burst in early 2000. Dot-com mania resembled just about every other stock speculation scheme that has sprouted from the roots of capitalism. The Internet was a new technology that was going to revolutionize business. Hundreds, perhaps thousands, of new companies were formed over night to exploit the Internet's potential. Investors poured significant amounts of money into the stock of these companies in an effort to get in on the ground floor. When all was said and done, the new dot-com firms could not deliver what they had promised. People came to realize that profits still had to be earned the old-fashioned way—by selling real products or services. When the bubble burst, telecommunications and Internet stock prices plummeted by more than 85 percent, and many firms went out of business.[19] Shareholders were left wondering what had happened to them.

A second wave of scandals hit the American economy in late 2001. Enron led the parade when it announced that it had overstated its profits. It soon became apparent not only that Enron's profits had evaporated, but also that executives had used creative accounting techniques to purposely mislead investors and regulators. Accounting giant Arthur Andersen was destroyed when its role in the Enron debacle became public. Enron was not the only company that had manipulated financial statements to mislead the investing public. Tyco, WorldCom, AOL Time Warner, Duke Energy, Global Crossing, Adelphia, and Freddie Mac are just a few examples of the major companies that were scandalized by accounting irregularities or whose top officers were accused of corruption. Ten Wall Street brokerage firms ended up agreeing to pay fines amounting to $1.4 billion for generating misleading investment reports to investors.[20] And, as happened when the dot-com bubble burst, investors ended up bearing the loss.

Fraud and corruption are ever present in a sinful world. I do not want to make light of that fact. Greed is a powerful force that can thrive in any economic system. But we need to recognize the inherent strengths and weaknesses of a given economic system that can encourage or hinder godly activities. The lack of material incentives plagues socialist economic systems. Uncontrolled greed can be an ongoing challenge for capitalist economies. Neither economic system offers the perfect environment for a business built on Christian principles. To be fair, we need to examine the deficiencies of the capitalist system in more detail.

The very real benefits of a market economy, discussed in chapter 2, pose some significant problems for Christians. Adam Smith, the Scottish professor of philosophy who is known as the father of modern economics, understood the benefits of a free market: "It is not from the benevolence of the butcher, the brewer, or the baker that we expect our dinner, but from their regard to their own interest.[21] . . . Every individual is continually exerting himself to find out the most advantageous employment for whatever capital he can command. . . . By directing that industry in such a manner as its produce may be of greatest, he intends only his own gain, and he is in this, as in many other cases, led by an invisible hand to promote an end which was no part his intention. Nor is it always the worse for the society that it was no part of it. By pursuing his own interest he frequently promotes that of the society more effectually than when he really intends to promote it." [22]

Smith introduced the radical notion that individuals, looking out for their own welfare, make decisions that collectively benefit society. Think of this example. I love dealing on cars. I am not good at it, but I enjoy trying to find the best deal that will save me the most money. I suspect that everyone else also wants to save money on his or her next car purchase. With everyone trying to get the best deal, companies cannot charge what they want. If they aren't competitive, consumers won't buy their cars. Even though the primary motivation of each individual consumer is to save as much money as possible, the collective benefit for society is lower prices for all cars. At least, the prices are lower than if car dealers could impose their own wills on the market.

An important point for Christians to keep in mind is that the pursuit of self-interest does not happen in a moral vacuum. Adam Smith recognized the potential abuses of an economic system that emphasized self-interest in pursuit of material pleasure. In his seminal work, *An Inquiry into the Nature and Causes of the Wealth of Nations*, Smith pointed out the dangers of greed and inequity. Workers whose sole motivation is to make more money are likely to "overwork themselves and to ruin their health and constitution in a few years."[23] Further, society must not ignore the plight of the poor. "No society can surely be flourishing and happy, of which the far greater part of the members are poor and miserable. It is but equity, besides, that they who feed, cloath and lodge the whole body of the people, should have such a share of the produce of their own labour as to be themselves tolerably well fed, cloathed and lodged."[24] Smith observed that while the poor and economically disadvantaged comprised most of the population, they still deserved a share of its material bounty.

To fully understand the relationship between self-interest and market behavior requires that we understand Smith's previous work, *The Theory of Moral Sentiments*. In this book Smith more fully described how morality shapes economic activity. Our primary goal in life is not to seek fame and fortune at the expense of others. "Humanity does not desire to be great, but to be beloved. It is not in being rich that truth and justice would rejoice, but in being trusted and believed."[25] This is not the picture of a greedy, self-centered economic actor. The self-interest that is so evident in *The Wealth of Nations* is framed by a sense of justice and the importance of being benevolent and sympathetic to others.[26] Restraining our own selfish desires and instead promoting the well being of others is, according to Smith, what gives us our humanity.[27]

Adam Smith was certainly aware that trying to apply the command "Love your neighbor as yourself" (Luke 10:27) does not come easily to man. In a market-dominated society that emphasizes individualism and self-interest, it becomes too easy for people to focus on their own sinful desires and pleasures. We are tempted to use the privacy of the impersonal market to engage in "every low profligacy and vice."[28] Because the marketplace is not always capable of promoting morality and civic virtues, government not only becomes necessary but desirable. According to Smith, "The civil magistrate is entrusted with the power not only of preserving the public peace by restraining injustice, but of promoting the prosperity of the commonwealth, by establishing good discipline, and by discouraging every sort of vice and impropriety."[29]

Christians can sympathize with Smith's view. Our society seems to have lost its moral underpinnings. Abortion is accepted as a way of life. Expressions of Christian values, such as the Ten Commandments, aren't allowed to be displayed in public buildings. Homosexuality is viewed as just another lifestyle. And the loss of society's moral underpinnings is evident in the world of business and economics.

The failure to base economic theory on a solid moral foundation frees the market from any constraints. The current debate on stem-cell research is a good example. Stem cells at the early stage have the potential to develop into any cell, tissue, or body part. Some feel that the stem cells found in human embryos hold the most promise. Our Christian concern is that in order to harvest these stem cells, the embryos must be destroyed. The ongoing political debate is over whether tax dollars should be used to fund such research. Largely ignored is the fact that private firms, which purchase human embryos or pay for eggs and sperm to make their own stem cells, are already harvesting embryonic stem cells. The market does not wait for ethical issues to be resolved. Lacking a consensus on the sanctity of human life, the market is free to allocate the building blocks of human life to the highest bidder.

Without moral constraints on the market, individual self-interest rules, and the accumulation of material possessions becomes more important than the well-being of society. Americans spent approximately $35 billion on alcoholic beverages in

1999,[30] but the federal government could only manage to budget $649 million on programs to ensure the safety of the nation's food supply.[31] Scarcity once meant that commodities like housing, food, or energy were in short supply. Today we view scarcity just like any other inconvenience that prevents us from living the lifestyle we think we deserve. Economics now treats the dilemma of not having a Wal-Mart ten minutes from your house the same as the inability to provide housing. Individualism appears to have replaced community in the United States.

Two thousand years ago, Christ told the parable of the rich fool. This was the story of the man who decided to build bigger barns to store his growing wealth so that he could live the good life. In Luke 12:21 Christ explained, "This is how it will be with anyone who stores up things for himself but is not rich toward God." The parable could just as well be describing America today. We want everything, and we want it now. Houses have grown from an average size of 950 square feet in 1950 to approximately 2,300 square feet today. Sport-utility vehicles are bigger than some pickup trucks, and a television with a screen of less than 25 inches is considered small. Capitalism is making it very easy for Americans to follow the path of the rich fool.

A sinister result of replacing moral values with self-interest is the way modern economic theory views labor. In economic terms, labor is human effort—the first of four economic resources. The other economic resources include land (all natural resources), capital (productive capacity), and entrepreneurial talent (risk taking). Modern economic theory requires that firms use the combination of economic resources that maximizes profit. The four categories are treated as variables in a mathematical equation that can be manipulated as needed to maximize profits. When self-interest takes the place of moral values, economic theory ignores the fact that human effort represents people and lives. In chapter 10 we will examine how firms use mergers, reorganization, or the courts to avoid paying promised benefits to employees.

In our relentless pursuit of efficiency, labor has no more value than a barrel of crude oil or the most advanced industrial computer. Managers plug the cost of each resource into a mathematical equation and look for the combination that produces the highest profit margin. In economic terms, this is called productive efficiency. In Scriptural terms, it is a disgrace. God did not create people to be just another economic resource. We are his prize creation. David wrote, "When I consider your heavens, the work of your fingers, the moon and the stars, which you have set in place, what is man that you are mindful of him, the son of man that you care for him? You made him a little lower than the heavenly beings and crowned him with glory and honor. You made him ruler over the works of your hands; you put everything under his feet: all flocks and herds, and the beasts of the field, the birds of the air, and the fish of the sea, all that swim the paths of the seas. O LORD, our Lord, how majestic is your name in all the earth!" (Psalm 8:3-9). David had it right. If God considered us lumps of coal, why would he spend so much time caring for us? Coal does not need a Savior to die for its sins so that it might be saved. God himself became our Savior. And God's Word makes it clear that humans should be treated with more respect than just another variable factor for economists to optimize.

Because they cherish life as a gift from God, Christians should not let economic theory or a market economy dictate practices that degrade human life. The International Labor Organization estimates that approximately 171 million children between the ages of 5 and 15[32] are engaged in work that jeopardizes [their] physical, mental, or moral well being.[33] These children are making products that we use every day, including clothes, food, and toys. The financial incentives to use children can be enormous. An investigative report of some two dozen American firms by the Associated Press in 1997 estimated that employers "saved $155 million in wages by hiring these under-age workers instead of people of legal age."[34] It is easy to ignore the consequences of our economic decisions. We get affordable and fashionable clothes without ever having to consider the processes that made them possible. The children that made it all possible are out of sight and out of mind.

The exploitation of children is deplorable. However, the larger point is that our economic choices have human implications. In Micah 2:2 we read, "They covet fields and seize them, and houses, and take them. They defraud a man of his home, a fellowman of his inheritance." When an economic system promotes or condones behavior that is contrary to the will of God, it has to be condemned. The removal of moral constraints from a capitalist economy encourages businesspeople to act on their sinful tendencies. Such behavior results in market abuses. Christians will want to keep the image of God firmly in focus so that they can conduct business in a way that treats all people with honesty and respect. But the issues are not always crystal clear.

Trying to determine who was right in the matter of the Gehl Company is not asking the right question. Both sides can make strong economic arguments for their positions. Christians need to appreciate the fact that the market will put immense pressure on them in its relentless pursuit of efficiency. It is too easy to dismiss management and investor decisions as examples of greed. This is not necessarily the case. There may be very sound economic reasons for those decisions. For the Christian, the motive is important. Equally important are the impacts that our decisions have on our fellow human beings. Managerial performance, investor decisions, and employee actions all need to be evaluated in this light.

FOUR

CHRIST
and capitalism

"In the beginning God created
the heavens and the earth."—*Genesis 1:1*

Whether or not an economic system is God pleasing depends on how it answers three fundamental questions:

- What goods and services should a society produce?
- How will those goods and services be produced?
- For whom will the goods and services be produced?

Although the Bible does not endorse a particular economic system, it does give very clear guidelines that help us evaluate an economic system. By applying scriptural principles to these three questions, we will be able to determine whether an economic system is God pleasing. The lessons learned by this exercise can help businesspeople review their own conduct in the economic marketplace.

Interestingly, we can find elements both of capitalism and socialism throughout Scripture. The essential elements of capitalism are clearly present in the Old Testament. Mosaic Law protected property rights and condemned unfair trade practices. Isaiah's denouncement of monopolistic practices implies that the established competitive market was being jeopardized. Within the local economic system, Scripture describes people as having different occupations and different financial means. Job is an example of a businessman who was richly blessed by God. He owned "seven thousand sheep, three thousand camels, five hundred yoke of oxen and five hundred donkeys, and had a large number of servants" (Job 1:3). We know that Israel was engaged in international commerce and became a rich and powerful nation during the reign of Solomon. Cedar for the temple was imported from Lebanon. Solomon's trading fleet carried Israeli agricultural products and copper to countries as far away as India and Africa. During the reign of Solomon, Israel developed artisans, craftsmen, and a vibrant merchant class.[1] These are just a few examples from the Old Testament that suggest that people owned property, specialized in different forms of employment, and traded in a competitive market.

Restraints on the competitive market are more pronounced in the New Testament. Jesus shows us that Christians should reach out with compassion toward the poor and vulnerable. His unmistakable message is that everything we have comes as a gift from God. He warns us about the competitive instincts that drive us to focus exclusively on our own well-beings. He encourages us to serve others and him with an attitude of gratefulness and thanksgiving. By reminding people of their obligation to pay their taxes, Christ also makes it clear that government has a legitimate role in society. The apostle Paul applied the teachings of Christ to real-world situations in the fledgling Christian church. Paul taught that Christians who are blessed with material wealth must not forget God. Blessed by success in the marketplace, Christian businesspeople will want to use their wealth to advance the work of the church.

While Christ and the apostle Paul are not advocating socialism, they are making it clear that capitalism has its limits. Christians engaged in commerce must not fall into the trap of maximizing profits at the expense of compromising their relationship with God. One way to stay out of that trap is to study these three fundamental questions in the context of God's Word.

What goods and services should a society produce?

From the very beginning, God's design for his creation was that people would work, not only to produce what was needed to sustain life but to provide for our happiness as well. In Genesis 2:15 we read, "The LORD God took the man and put him in the Garden of Eden to work it and take care of it." God didn't do this because he needed a caretaker. Quite to the contrary. He wanted to give each person's life meaning and pleasure. "I realized that it is good and proper for a man to eat and drink, and to find satisfaction in his toilsome labor under the sun during the few days of life God has given him—for this is his lot. Moreover, when God gives any man wealth and possessions, and enables him to enjoy them, to accept his lot and be happy in his work—this is a gift of God" (Ecclesiastes 5:18,19).

It is part of God's plan that we should work his creation and, in so doing, find gladness, reward, and sustenance. As Martin Luther explained, "I believe that God created me and all that exists, and that he gave me my body and soul, eyes, ears, and all my members, my mind and all my abilities."

Luther continued, "And I believe that God still preserves me by richly and daily providing clothing and shoes, food and drink, property and home, spouse and children, land, cattle, and all I own, and all I need to keep my body and life."[2] God created all things for a purpose. He wants and expects us to produce material goods and services that are blessings to his people and glorify his name.

God gave humans authority over his creation. That doesn't give us the right to use that authority for sinful purposes. A society that condones lying, cheating, stealing, the production of pornography, and the production of music that promotes violence is not contributing to the common good or respecting God's will. A 1997 *US News and World Report* article estimated that Americans were spending roughly $8 billion annually on adult videos.[3] That number has probably not declined since then. Through human choice, an economy may produce the goods and services that the society demands. But when moral values are removed from the economic equation, the goods and services a society chooses to produce may not be God pleasing. Spending billions on pornography can in no way glorify God's name.

Many other factors determine the goods and services a society produces. Work performed by members of a society does not, by itself, improve the economic well-being of the society. Economists teach that wages paid to an employee are directly related to that employee's productivity. Of course, labor supply conditions and training costs also are important. But let's focus on productivity. If Dick can build 20 Sony PlayStations per hour and is paid $10 per hour, Sony is getting two PlayStations for every dollar it pays Dick. Because Sony is a profit-maximizing firm, the company is contemplating moving its production facility to a foreign country because the wage rate in that country is $4 per hour. Should Sony take advantage of the lower wage rate in the foreign country? The answer depends on the productivity of that particular labor market. If the foreign employee can only produce four PlayStations per hour, Sony is getting one PlayStation per labor dollar spent. Sony will get more PlayStations per dollar by keeping Dick on the payroll.

When a society spends economic resources on goods and services that do not increase productivity, all of society will suffer. Drug and alcohol abuse has been estimated to cost American business $98.5 billion annually in lost productivity and related expenses.[4] Likewise, the US spends $19.2 billion annually fighting the war on drugs.[5] Spending money on drug use or drug prevention does not result in more goods and services that society can use and enjoy. Instead, it siphons off money that could be invested in worker training, health care, new roads, technology, or a host of products and services that would increase the productive capacity of the economy. Abusing drugs is not only contrary to God's will, but it also hurts society in a number of ways. Economic output is just one example.

As mentioned earlier, free-market proponents minimize the role that government can play in the economic life of the nation. In their opinion, the best that government can do is just stand aside and let the market sort things out to produce whatever society demands.

Though centralized planning may not be needed, to dismiss the role of government in the economic life of a country is shortsighted. We might also question such a position on the basis of Scripture.

Governments are a gift from God. When the apostle Paul spoke about the reason for our obedience to the government, he said, "Everyone must submit himself to the governing authorities, for there is no authority except that which God has established. The authorities that exist have been established by God" (Romans 13:1). Peter explained the purpose of governments when he wrote that governments "punish those who do wrong and . . . commend those who do right" (1 Peter 2:14). Like it or not, those statements allow governments a great deal of discretion. Government involvement in providing goods and services such as defense, education, and health care is neither promoted nor prohibited by Scripture. If a government chooses to provide these benefits, we should not automatically dismiss such involvement as unscriptural.

Furthermore, the government does have an explicit role to play in maintaining a level economic playing field. In Exodus 20:15 God is very clear when he says, "You shall not steal." Christians understand that all property ultimately belongs to God. But that statement shows that God gives us the privilege of owning private property—a privilege that is central to a market-based economic system. God also gives the government authority to punish those who break the law by stealing. Peter's comments about the government's role in punishing wrongdoers (1 Peter 2:14) show that the government can punish lawbreakers as it sees fit. Enforcing rules that have economic ramifications is a scripturally legitimate function of government.

In other places, the Scriptures speak of policies that affect a country's economic system. In Isaiah 5:8 the prophet writes, "Woe to you who add house to house and join field to field till no space is left and you live alone in the land." As we have seen, if a free-market system is to work efficiently, competition is a prerequisite. The government helps to maintain a healthy economy by promoting antimonopolistic policies that ensure free, open, and competitive markets.

In Leviticus chapter 19, Moses outlined a number of other statutes that form the foundation for government policies involving a nation's economy. "Do not deceive one another. Do not defraud your neighbor" (verses 11,13). A free market works when all players have access to equal information. A car dealer who rolls back the odometers to make his cars look more valuable than they really are would have an unfair advantage over other dealers—but his customers would pay the price. If a tax accountant promised to save her clients money, but did so by cheating the IRS, her clients might pay a very high price. In the end, those businesses might hurt themselves more than others because consumers would learn to avoid them. Laws that promote the free flow of information can be God pleasing and economically beneficial.

Later in Leviticus chapter 19, Moses wrote, "Do not use dishonest standards when measuring length, weight or quantity" (verse 35). Capitalism depends on free exchange. It is imperative that the market be fair. Because the government ensures that the scales at the butcher shop, the gas pump at the filling station, and the survey for the land that you own are accurate, consumers do not have to spend extra time and dollars double-checking their purchases. Accuracy in weights and measures improves economic efficiency.

Some of the biblical injunctions that influence the economy have nothing to do with fairness or efficiency, however. Modern economic theory heavily stresses the need for increasing economic growth and efficiency. But focusing exclusively on materialism ignores the scriptural command to spend economic resources on such nonmoney-making activities as evangelism and Bible study. Christ's plan for us is to spread his Word. "Go and make disciples of all nations, baptizing them in the name of the Father and of the Son and of the Holy Spirit, and teaching them to obey everything I have commanded you" (Matthew 28:19,20). We do this out of love and respect for God. One way we do this is through our offerings. The apostle Paul wrote in 2 Corinthians 9:7, "Each man should give what he has decided in his heart to give, not reluctantly or under compulsion, for God loves a cheerful giver." Christians don't use economic resources such as time and money exclusively for production. They use those resources—sometimes at a substantial sacrifice—for the spiritual and physical well-being of God's prize creation. As Christians, our primary goal is not to increase our material wealth but to glorify God.

How should goods and services be produced?

With words that give us a new perspective regarding the things we have, the psalmist reminds us that our resources are gifts entrusted to us by God. "You made him ruler over the works of your hands; you put everything under his feet: all flocks and herds, and the beasts of the field, the birds of the air, and the fish of the sea, all that swim the paths of the seas (Psalm 8:6-8). Instead of worrying about obtaining material possessions, we are encouraged, by the Scriptures, to be wise stewards of the resources God has entrusted to us. Hoarding of resources is not condoned. In James 5:2,3 we read: "Your wealth has rotted, and moths have eaten your clothes. Your gold and silver are corroded. Their corrosion will testify against you and eat your flesh like fire. You have hoarded wealth in the last days." Christians glorify God by managing the resources he has given us to further his kingdom.

As we go about our business, we must not lose sight of the privilege God has given us to manage our resources. Some people question whether the earth can sustain continued economic growth or whether we will exhaust the resources of this planet. The Kyoto Summit, called to address the problem of global warming, highlighted some dangers that the earth faces. If we don't manage our resources well, we will suffer along with the environment.

Love Canal is probably one of the earliest and most infamous examples of how pollution can harm human health.

Located on an old chemical waste dump near Niagara Falls, Love Canal was redeveloped into a school and residential neighborhood. In the late 1970s, residents began experiencing adverse health effects. A subsequent investigation revealed that the buried hazardous chemicals were leaking into the groundwater that the residents were drinking. In the end the federal government spent millions of dollars relocating residents and cleaning up the site.[6]

Almost daily we hear news reports that raise questions about the health of our environment. The rain forests are being destroyed. Another species will soon be extinct. Some parts of the world are unable to raise enough food to support their populations for the rest of the 21st century. These are legitimate concerns, but they do not mean that the earth is going to end up looking like the moon. In 1950, one farmer could produce enough food to support 13 people. Today, with the help of advanced technology and research, that same farmer can support 110 people.[7] The extinction of animals because of overharvesting also can be corrected without excessive sacrifice. Botswana, Zimbabwe, and South Africa allow for the private ownership of African elephants. This has increased the number of elephants in their countries while overall herd numbers in the rest of Africa have dropped.[8]

Economic theory fails to acknowledge that our gracious and mighty Lord is always in control. Economists look at individual effort and work that generate an economic reward. Through the production of goods and services, society is materially improved. For Christians this is only part of the story. In Deuteronomy 28:9-14 Moses reminded the Israelites that God would be the source of their prosperity. Their main concern was to be that their lives—including their business dealings—glorified God:

> The LORD will establish you as his holy people, as he promised you on oath, if you keep the commands of the LORD your God and walk in his ways. Then all the peoples on earth will

see that you are called by the name of the LORD, and they will fear you. The LORD will grant you abundant prosperity—in the fruit of your womb, the young of your livestock and the crops of your ground—in the land he swore to your forefathers to give you.

The LORD will open the heavens, the storehouse of his bounty, to send rain on your land in season and to bless all the work of your hands. You will lend to many nations but will borrow from none. The LORD will make you the head, not the tail. If you pay attention to the commands of the LORD your God that I give you this day and carefully follow them, you will always be at the top, never at the bottom. Do not turn aside from any of the commands I give you today, to the right or to the left, following other gods and serving them.

Notice God's promise to bless them with prosperity (verse 13).
As Christians, we will always view our participation in the economic system in the context of God's Word and promises. Out of thanks for the rich blessings God has bestowed upon us, we will want to work and honor our God. The Bible shows us how we will do this. Owning land or making money by employing people is not discouraged. In Luke 10:7 we read, "The worker deserves his wages." Nothing in Scripture suggests to us that economic production through the use of labor is wrong. However, the exploitation of those resources for gain is sinful. When business abuses God's prized creation to satisfy its own greed, such economic policies are on a collision course with God's will.
This does not mean that all workers should receive the same rewards. In fact, those who refuse to work should receive no reward at all (2 Thessalonians 3:10). The book of Proverbs echoes that thought: "Laziness brings on deep sleep, and the shiftless man goes hungry" (19:15). Contrast this to 22:29: "Do

you see a man skilled in his work? He will serve before kings; he will not serve before obscure men." Those with greater ambition and skill will be rewarded accordingly.

For whom should the goods and services be produced?

In a market economy, price determines how goods and services will be allocated. My son would like a new printer for his computer. He would have one by now if it were not for the price. Our economy produces a plethora of printers, but only those who can afford the retail prices will buy them. Some people are able to enjoy goods and services that others can't.

That people will occupy different stations in society is taken for granted in Scripture. The apostle Paul wrote, "Slaves, obey your earthly masters with respect and fear, and with sincerity of heart, just as you would obey Christ. Serve wholeheartedly, as if you were serving the Lord, not men, because you know that the Lord will reward everyone for whatever good he does, whether he is slave or free" (Ephesians 6:5,7,8). This statement implies that different people will have different economic capabilities. The important point is not whether or not we have as much as our neighbor but whether or not our focus is on the Lord. God's primary concern is not how material resources are allocated but that we do not allow those material blessings to interfere with our relationship with him.

The fact that there will always be different stations in society, however, doesn't release us from our obligation to help those who cannot help themselves. Because we live at a time of wealth and prosperity, we may be tempted to view the poor and unfortunate as lazy slackers. But the Scriptures are full of encouragement to help those in need. In Ephesians 4:28 the apostle Paul wrote, "He who has been stealing must steal no longer, but must work, doing something useful with his own hands, that he may have something to share with those in need." One of the reasons God has blessed us with the resources we have is so that we might help those in need. Paul spent a great deal of time raising money for less fortunate Christians in Jerusalem. If we need more proof about the importance of charitable giving, we can look at Christ's own words as he instructs us to help the poor. In Matthew 6:1-4 Christ makes it clear that we are not only to help the needy but also that our motivations for providing that help should be pure. Christians in business will not use charitable giving as a marketing or public relations tool. Instead, Christian businesspersons will help those in need because faith in God inspires their service to one another.

A God-pleasing economic system will answer the three fundamental economic questions in a way that keeps Christ at the center of our thoughts, words, and deeds. Manufacturing goods and services that contradict the will of God is wasteful, even if there is strong consumer demand and healthy profit potential. Utilizing production methods that exploit people, callously destroy the environment, or reflect the lack of trust in the omnipotence of our Lord fail to adequately address the second fundamental economic question. A resource allocation system that distributes scarce resources in a way that ignores the plight of the most needy and vulnerable in society is suspect.

FIVE
A CHRISTIAN critique of market economics

"It is easier for a camel to go through the eye of a needle than for a rich man to enter the kingdom of God."
—*Jesus Christ (Matthew 19:24)*

Paul eloquently described the Christian's attitude toward business and economics in 1 Timothy 6:6-10. "Godliness with contentment is great gain. For we brought nothing into the world, and we can take nothing out of it. But if we have food and clothing, we will be content with that. People who want to get rich fall into temptation and a trap and into many foolish and harmful desires that plunge men into ruin and destruction. For the love of money is a root of all kinds of evil. Some people, eager for money, have wandered from the faith and pierced themselves with many griefs." But sometimes it seems that the Christian's attitude toward economics is at odds with accepted economic policies or goals. In this chapter we will focus on some specific problems that government and markets pose for Christians competing in the marketplace. We will see that the government can introduce economic inefficiencies into the market that encourage sinful behavior. We will also learn that the market is not always an appropriate tool for allocating resources.

Markets work because they are impersonal and value free, and they promote self-interest. Each consumer is expected to look out for his or her own welfare. My goal as the seller is to get the most that I can for my product. The consumer wants to pay no more than absolutely necessary. Both of us have our own self-interest in mind. As a business owner, I need to maximize my profit in order to cover my costs and provide for my family. If I am more worried about my customers than my own welfare, I might sell for less and reduce my profits. In that case, customers would be made better off, but my family and I would be worse off. Economic efficiency would not be achieved.

The market not only promotes individual self-interest; the market is also impersonal. When I was growing up on a farm in central Wisconsin, my dad did quite a bit of business at a feed mill in a small town approximately five miles away. The proprietor was a jack-of-all-trades and, contrary to the old adage, was quite proficient in each of them. He was a plumber, an electrician, and an implement dealer, in addition to operating the feed mill. Some people thought that his products were priced too high. A farmer could often purchase the same product from a large farm supply store in a distant city for less than he could at the local mill. But if you bought your supplies through the local mill, the owner always seemed to be there whenever you needed service. On more than one occasion, he helped us out in a pinch.

My dad could have bought his supplies anywhere. That is the nature of the market. Sellers and buyers are the means to an end. When they stop satisfying one another, the commercial relationship is terminated. Self-interest forces the market participants to focus on price. The impersonal nature of business reinforces the old adage: Friends are friends, but business is business.

In addition to being impersonal, markets are value free. Once you purchase an item, you can do with it as you please. I remember an article in the January 7, 2001, *Milwaukee Journal Sentinel*.[1] An elderly couple had owned a building on a street corner in Milwaukee, Wisconsin. They sold the building to a couple of gentlemen who planned to operate a bar on the premises. The first thing the new owners did was paint the entire building "midnight violet." While the owners basked in the glory of their freshly painted building, the neighbors were less than impressed. Unfortunately for the neighbors, there was very little that they could do. Lacking any legal prohibitions, the owners were free to paint the building any color they chose. The marketplace does not care what a buyer does with the product. The only stipulation is the asking price. Once that is paid, the market moves on to the next transaction.

While markets may allow for the efficient transaction of commercial deals, the market is not prepared to handle all economic transactions. Certain goods and services simply are not meant to be traded in a marketplace. Economists differentiate between private goods that can be efficiently traded in markets and public goods that are less adaptable to market transactions. The major difference between the two goods is illustrated by the concepts of *exclusivity* and *rivals*. Benefits from *exclusive* goods can be limited to the purchaser. Goods are *rivals* when the consumption of the good reduces the amount available for other people to consume. Gasoline is an example. The benefits of gasoline are limited to the purchaser. And once the gasoline has been burned, it is gone forever.

Some products or services simply don't seem appropriate for trade on the free market. An example might be human organs. Do we want the free market to allocate who will get a liver transplant? Certainly the impersonal nature of the market would eliminate the political bias that sometimes creeps into the current allocation system.

We only have to think back to the example of Mickey Mantle to understand how political transplant decisions can be. Mantle, who had been a heavy drinker, needed a liver transplant if he were to survive. The question was whether a person who destroyed his liver through the abuse of alcohol should get a new one. While not all the details were publicized, his story made headlines, and he received a new liver. In an impersonal market, name recognition would not matter, but other obvious problems would arise. Selling organs to the highest bidder quickly comes to mind.

A humorous example that demonstrates another limitation of the market when allocating certain goods and services can be found in the movie *Brewster's Millions*. In this movie Richard Pryor has to spend $30 million in 30 days in order to collect a far larger inheritance. The catch is that his purchases can have no economic value. In one instance, Pryor spends a small fortune on a very rare postage stamp. The antagonists were delighted because they knew the stamp was worth money and, therefore, didn't meet the conditions of the contest. They were delighted, that is, until they realized that Pryor had informed them of his purchase by sending a postcard with the rare stamp affixed. Since the post office had cancelled the stamp, it no longer had value. Markets do not regulate the use of a product or service. Once the price has been paid, the market stops caring.

The tendency of modern economic theory to be value neutral has allowed the twin gods of self-interest and materialism to supplant Christian morals as the bases for economic decisions and practices. Consequently, free-market economics have been corrupted by the sinful desires of man. We see this in the way we manage the resources God has given us.

Too many of us believe that the material blessings we enjoy result from our own efforts. Once we taste material success, Satan uses greed to change our attitude from one that trusts in the Lord to one that covets more material wealth. Soon we find it easier to give less and less to the church or those in need. We justify our stinginess with excuses that we are experiencing a poor business climate or that we need to save for a rainy day. Or we defend ourselves with the accusation that the church will waste the money on frivolous projects anyway. God is not fooled by our self-righteous proclamation that we have worked hard and thus deserve all that we have earned. Everything we have is from the Lord. He rightfully expects us to use our material wealth not only to support our families and ourselves but also to help those in need and to advance the mission of the church. Our Lord makes it abundantly clear that our stinginess is offensive. In Malachi 3:8 the Lord spoke through the prophet: "Will a man rob God? Yet you rob me. But you ask, 'How do we rob you?' In tithes and offerings." Christians will not use the excuse that "business is slow" as a reason for not giving generously to God. Instead, Christian businesspeople will see the poor widow described in Mark 12:41-44 as an example of a person who shows us that we have every reason to give cheerfully to the Lord no matter what we have.

When we allow the economic principle of self-interest to be the motivation for our economic decisions, we lose sight of the fact that everything we call our own is a gift from God. Economists want us to believe that we will be rewarded based on how the market values our contributions. This explains why the very talented Tiger Woods makes millions playing golf while I, with almost no talent, earn considerably less. However, God makes it clear in Scripture that he, and not the market, is the final arbiter of who will be blessed and who will go hungry. The Lord promises in Malachi 3:10,11, "'Bring the whole tithe into the storehouse, that there may be food in my house. Test me in this,' says the LORD Almighty, 'and see if I will not throw open the floodgates of heaven and pour out so much blessing that you will not have room enough for it. I will prevent pests from devouring your crops, and the vines in your fields will not cast their fruit,' says the LORD Almighty." We need to understand that the economic system is simply a tool that God uses to distribute his blessings.

Because of our weak sinful nature, we as Christians in business often forget that we can trust our Lord. I find it amazing that so many of us seem to act as if God isn't present when we go to work. We recite the Apostles' or Nicene Creed every week. In those statements we acknowledge awesome truths that we cannot see or even know on our own. That is, we confess that by the grace of God we are saved through faith in Christ Jesus. If we truly believe God on an issue of such monumental importance, can we not trust his promises to bless us as we glorify him through our business decisions? We know how to apply God's Word to our lives at home, school, and play. We shouldn't be afraid to apply his Word to our lives at work as well.

By overemphasizing self-interest as the goal of our economic decisions, Americans have also eroded the moral authority of government to act. Government is seen as inefficient and corrupted by special interest groups. Many believe that private markets should have exclusive rights to allocate scarce resources. Milwaukee voters expressed support for this view by electing a school board that allows private charter and parochial schools to compete with the public school system for students. The school choice program in Milwaukee gives disadvantaged families cash payments so that they can enroll their children in alternative schools. Supporters of school choice argue that by opening education to competition, the quality of education in public schools, and ultimately in all schools, will improve.

Even the federal government has embraced the idea of market efficiency. The Environmental Protection Agency (EPA), through the Chicago Board of Trade, sells the right to pollute to the electric utility industry.[2] The EPA sets minimum acceptable air standards that are used to determine how much pollution can be discharged into the atmosphere. Companies are given an allowance or pollution quota that sets the maximum amount of emissions they can legally release into the atmosphere. For example, a power plant may be allowed to discharge two tons of sulfur dioxide (a major component of acid rain) per year into the atmosphere. The allowances are a marketable security that can be bought or sold. Non-polluting power plants can sell their rights to pollute to those companies that cannot meet their quotas. Supply and demand sets the price. In theory the market will encourage companies to improve the efficiency of their power plants by making the cost of polluting prohibitively expensive. Economists would like to see the program expanded so that the government wouldn't even have to establish pollution standards.

Although by replacing government regulations with market economics we may effectively achieve our public policy goals, the practice is not without its own dangers. Sin often distorts the market in ways that embarrass Christians and grieve God. The slave trade in pre–Civil War America is an example of how

53

a market can result in the sinful allocation of resources. We learned in chapter 3 that if an economic system degrades human life, that system is suspect. Strong profit motive and intense self-interest drove many slave owners to use capitalism sinfully to buy and sell human beings. The market for abortions is another example of how sin often distorts a market. As long as there is sin, there will be demand for abortions. Given sufficient demand, there will always be those doctors who are willing to perform abortions for profit. The market will not stop abortions on ethical grounds.

Economists are quick to praise the profit motive as the primary motivating force for achieving economic efficiency. But that profit motive obviously has a dark side. Ivan Boesky—the late, great, junk-bond trader—once said, "Greed is all right by the way. I want you to know that. I think greed is healthy. You can be greedy and still feel good about yourself."[3] The apostle Paul's message was quite different: "The love of money is a root of all kinds of evil" (1 Timothy 6:10).

Boesky ended up spending time in jail for insider trading. Essentially, he placed himself and his own interests above the interests of his clients in order to make more money for himself. Ivan Boesky was not the first to do this, and he will not be the last. The point is that markets are subject to the same sinful pressures as any other human institutions.

God created the government, not the market, to maintain order in society. In certain situations, markets are not the appropriate mechanism for guiding human behavior. Selling pollution allowances is an innovative way to link the profit motive with self-interest in a way that benefits society and diminishes the need for government intervention. But Paul reminds us of an incontrovertible fact in Romans 3:23: "All have sinned and fall short of the glory of God." We can see the clear evidence that sin has thoroughly permeated our nature, that sin warps our reliance on self-interest. Greed so easily becomes our primary focus. Whenever our sinful passions take over and we begin to employ the market for wicked purposes, the government should become engaged in the marketplace.

Because of the inefficiency of markets in certain situations, however, the government can also become guilty of wasting economic resources and encouraging sinful behavior. If the government-operated school system fails to educate the youth, alternatives need to be explored. When the government subsidizes people for not working, Christians should be concerned. The Great Society programs of Lyndon Johnson were created with good intentions. Eliminating poverty is a noble and God-pleasing goal. However, the evidence indicates that instead of alleviating poverty, welfare made the poor even more dependent on the government. Christians once again have reason to seek changes. Government is not the answer for all social ills.

Christians are not value free. We are not able to engage in commerce as if nothing more important than profit were at stake. Our eternal life should be reason enough to set a higher standard of conduct in the marketplace. As Christians, we will look to the cross for guidance in everything we do, including how we conduct our business affairs. We understand that self-interest is a powerful motivator, but it is one that is tempered by having a servant's attitude. Material comforts are worthy goals as long as they do not become idols that replace our devotion to the triune God. Christians in business can, and must, make conscious efforts to be the "light of the world" that Christ describes in Matthew 5:14.

SIX

CAPITALISM and compassion

"Let no one ever come to you without leaving better and happier."—*Mother Teresa*

Nearly 24 million people with work-limiting disabilities live in the United States.[1] Approximately nine million are too disabled to work.[2] The majority of the rest work part time or hold temporary positions. Unemployment rates for workers with disabilities are significantly higher than for other workers. It should come as no surprise then that the disabled are more likely than workers without disabilities to be classified as poor.[3] The fact is that people with disabilities are often dependent on the government or other social programs for financial support.

On August 22, 1996, President Clinton signed into law a bill that overhauled the nation's welfare program. Wisconsin's version of this law is known as Wisconsin Works, or W-2. Basically, the new program requires work in exchange for government assistance. The maximum length of time people can receive cash assistance is generally limited to five years.[4]

The change in the nation's welfare program received bipartisan support. Many people believed that the old system encouraged people not to work. Others felt that welfare undermined the family and the norms and values of "marriage, work, education, and self-control."[5] Whatever the perception, requiring people to work in exchange for government assistance represented a major shift in public policy.

Most of us know someone who is developmentally disabled and may not be able to earn a living. Most Americans believe that requiring people to work in exchange for government assistance makes sense. For Christians, those two observations create tension. How do we show compassion for those in need but still maintain policies that encourage the able-bodied to work? Complicating this task is the fact that being compassionate and being competitive in the marketplace are not always complementary goals.

As we have seen in earlier chapters, market competition yields significant tangible benefits. By encouraging each of us to maximize our potential, society benefits materially. But business is not a social welfare agency. Its primary purpose is to convert economic resources into goods and services for people. Competition forces business to be very efficient at this task. But what happens to people who, through no fault of their own, lack the skills or intellectual capability to compete in the marketplace? I know a young lady with Down's syndrome. She doesn't possess the physical and mental gifts to compete with the "average" person for a high-paying job. Are we going to relegate her to a life of poverty because the market does not value her talents? Christians need to carefully review how they balance the need for compassion and the need to remain competitive.

As citizens of the United States, we have been richly blessed with material wealth. Christians know that with wealth comes responsibility. It is too easy to compartmentalize our faith and ignore what is going on around us. The parable of the good Samaritan reminds us that we have an obligation to look out for our neighbor. Reflecting the love of our Savior, who sacrificed himself for us, we are glad to look out for our neighbor. But how we do that in a competitive, market-based economy becomes a thorny issue.

The prophet Jeremiah stated a profound and humbling truth that helps us recognize the value of human life: "Before I formed you in the womb I knew you, before you were born I set you apart" (Jeremiah 1:5). We may not be able to begin to fathom the depth of this truth. But when we apply Jeremiah's observation to our business practices, his words give us pause. Not only were we created in God's image, but God has known us from eternity. We have a special place in his creation. People must not be treated as another commodity used to further the interests of an individual, business, or society. When economic motivations drive people to abort babies, euthanize the elderly, or exploit labor to enhance profits, the economic system is suspect. Whether a nation's economic system is socialist or capitalist, if economic gain replaces God and his Word as our focus, our focus is wrong. The parable of the rich fool (Luke 12:15-21) drives home this point.

Capitalism, as practiced in America today, emphasizes self-interest without considering the impact on the community. Even the United States Army emphasizes personal self-interest when its advertisements suggest that you should "be all that you can be." Our heavenly Father reminds us not to focus exclusively on our own needs and wants. In Jeremiah 9:24 we are told that we have a Lord who values kindness, justice, and righteousness. Christ adds to this by making it clear that the primary motivation for all that we do must first be to honor and love our heavenly Father and concomitantly to love our neighbor (Matthew 22:37-39). The noted theologian Thomas Aquinas observed that we can find perfect happiness in God alone. However, he proposed that because we have neighbors, our love for God will automatically spill over into our relationships with them.[6] Our personal talents may be prized and regarded in the marketplace, but we must still recognize that our love for God will propel us to genuinely care about the plights of others in our society.

Our Founding Fathers tried to capture the delicate balance between the benefits of individualism and the need to create a sense of unity when they established this country. "We hold these truths to be self-evident, that all men are created equal, that they are endowed by their Creator with certain unalienable Rights, that among these are Life, Liberty and the pursuit of Happiness." With these words the delegates of the Second Continental Congress declared America's independence from Britain and their own intent to form a nation that protected the people from an overbearing government. The intent spelled out in the Declaration is still a worthy goal. To achieve that goal, however, requires more than just political freedom. In order for all the citizens to be able to earn a living and support a family, they must all have the opportunity to benefit from the fruits of a market economy. Discrimination not only hurts people economically, but it breeds political resentment that harms all of society.

We do not have to look far to find examples of people who take advantage of the less fortunate in the marketplace. A few years ago we learned that credit card companies were starting to target the mentally challenged with credit card solicitations. Fierce competition for cardholders has led some companies to look for groups of people that may have been ignored in the past. The obvious problem is that not all individuals with mental handicaps are capable of handling credit cards. Because they may not be able to understand the concept of credit or to comprehend what it means to live within a budget, these people are especially vulnerable to credit card marketers. After getting their cards, some have run up huge debts that they cannot possibly repay. As Christians in business, we need to understand that not all of our customers have the same level of sophistication that we possess. The Christian businessperson needs to look out for the weak and vulnerable and to make sure he or she doesn't exploit them.

The Christian response to help those in need does not stop at our borders. A story in the June 23, 2001, *Milwaukee Journal Sentinel* revealed that slave labor was being used to harvest the cocoa beans that major firms such as Hershey's and Nestlé were using to produce chocolate.[7] The United States State Department estimated that approximately 15,000 boys between the ages of 9 and 12 had been sold into slavery. A slave could be purchased for as little as $35. Slaves were beaten regularly. They were forced to work 12-hour days. They were undernourished.[8] What obligation did American firms and consumers have to rectify this situation?

Christian businesspeople are concerned about the weak and vulnerable. But not exploiting them is only part of the equation. In 2003, 35.9 million Americans lived in poverty.[9] Approximately 45 million didn't have health insurance. That is up from 43.6 million in 2002.[10] By 2012 it is estimated that Americans will spend approximately $445.9 billion on prescription drugs. That is up from $140.6 billion in 2001.[11] Some people have to make choices between purchasing medication or food. In one of the world's richest democracies, is it acceptable that so many people are poor or go without health care?

Americans have always prided themselves on being self-reliant. From the early settlers on the western frontier to modern corporate warriors, Americans have placed a premium on personal responsibility and initiative. That attitude complements a capitalist economic system. The division of labor found in free-market economies allows each individual to become specialized in a specific trade or occupation. Henry Ford's assembly line is a classic example. By developing the assembly line, he was able to produce cars cheaply and at a rate never before imagined. The key was to have each worker perform one job task instead of building an entire car.

Such specialization has been incorporated throughout our entire economy. For example, doctors can spend more time expanding their knowledge and improving their surgical skills because they don't need to worry about planting a garden or milking a cow to get their food and drink. As a result, the economy has become even more productive. Our store shelves are filled with a greater array of products than ever before.

An economy based on the specialization of labor exhibits its own set of weaknesses, however. The specialization of labor combined with our penchant for individualism has resulted in a society that has lost its sense of community. Examples of this are easy to find. When I was growing up in central Wisconsin, my family and I knew all of our neighbors. For some in my neighborhood, going to church was like a family reunion. My grandparents, who lived in town, knew everyone on their block. And family members took care of one another. My grandparents, for example, took care of my great-grandmother.

She lived with them for a couple of months out of the year and then another child took his or her turn. Times have changed. My parents lament the fact that the old neighbors no longer live in the neighborhood. When I drive down my grandparents' street, I don't know anybody who lives there. In church, the number of new faces is staggering. I probably know fewer than 25 percent of the people. The sad thing is that I am part of the problem. During the 12 years I worked in retail, I lived in six different towns in five states. Today I don't know a single neighbor on my street. And as families have moved apart, they have lost some of the sense of connection. Nursing homes have taken over the role of caring for our elderly parents.

To a certain degree, economics contributes to the loss of community. Businesses, looking for new markets or lower operating costs, are quite willing to force people to move in order to keep their jobs. A friend of mine worked for GM in Janesville, Wisconsin. The company opened a new plant in Fort Wayne, Indiana, and was threatening to close the Janesville plant. Any employees who transferred to the new plant were able to retain their seniority and avoid a possible layoff. My friend moved, but GM never closed the Janesville plant. I suspect GM, wishing to open its new plant with a core of experienced employees, used the threat of a plant closure to get some employees to move. In any event, constant relocations from town to town make it difficult for people to establish a sense of community.

Along with the sense of community, I have lost the sense of commitment to my neighbor's well-being that my parents had and their parents had before them. Because I am generally ignorant of the welfare of my fellow citizens, I am able to ignore the plight of those I choose not to acknowledge. I know that I am not alone.

I know too that America's me-first attitude is not God pleasing. Many times in the Scriptures, the Lord shows us that we are to be concerned about the poor and those in need. In Leviticus 19:9,10 God told the people to leave some of the harvest at the edge of the fields and not to go over the vineyard

61

a second time so that the poor would be able to eat. Later (25:13), God commanded that in the Year of Jubilee (once every 50 years) the land be returned to the original owners. Some have suggested that one reason for the Year of Jubilee was that the Lord wanted to discourage the accumulation of property to the detriment of the poor. Through Zechariah the Lord commands, "Administer true justice; show mercy and compassion to one another. Do not oppress the widow or the fatherless, the alien or the poor. In your hearts do not think evil of each other"(7:9,10). And Jesus condemned the rich man in the parable of the rich fool (Luke 12:15-21). The rich man amassed so much wealth that he tore down his small barns to build larger structures. His plan was to gain enough wealth so he would not have to work. But God took his life. Christ ends that parable by saying, "This is how it will be with anyone who stores up things for himself but is not rich toward God" (verse 21). These words remind us that we focus too much on ourselves.

To remedy this problem, some people suggest that we should provide everyone with the opportunity to enjoy certain human rights. "First among these are the rights to life, food, clothing, shelter, rest, medical care, and basic education. . . . In order to ensure these necessities, all persons have a right to earn a living, which for most people in our economy is through remunerative employment. All persons also have the right to security in the event of sickness, unemployment and old age. . . . as well as the right to healthful working conditions, to wages and other benefits sufficient to provide individuals and families with a standard of living in keeping with human dignity, and to the possibility of property ownership."[12]

Guaranteeing these rights to every person sounds good but does not make economic or scriptural sense.[13] As we saw earlier, a market economy will not provide everything everyone desires. Economists assign a value to labor according to the amount that labor contributes to the production of a good or service. Value is determined by the price consumers are willing to pay. No one in his or her right mind would pay $800 for a milk shake. And the owner of the ice cream stand will not pay for a person to make those milk shakes if no one will buy them. Since most people will not pay more than $5 for the shake, the labor and other resources can't exceed $5. No matter how talented the employee, his or her wage won't go higher than the price the owner receives for the product.

Labor is an extremely important part of the economic equation. The human being, God's prize creation, is the only one who can transform the earth's resources into useable products. A tree will always be a tree until it dies. People alone can take the tree and transform it into a 2 by 4, a picture frame, a wagon, or any of an unlimited number of other products. Because we have this unique ability, our efforts should be valued differently than natural resources like coal and oil. In a market economy, the question is whether it is possible to guarantee all people an acceptable standard of living no matter what value the market might put on their labor.

Scripture and economic theory both reject the tantalizingly seductive notion of guaranteeing all people wages that would allow them to live a certain lifestyle. Economic efficiency and the subsequent material improvement are achieved only through competition. Discount retailing provides us with an example. In 1962 Kmart was one of the first companies to introduce discount retailing. What we now take for granted was quite innovative back then. A square box was filled up with an incredibly wide selection of everyday consumable staples like soap, oil filters, and socks. Operating on volume, Kmart was able to offer these products at lower prices than grocery or variety stores. By 1995 the discount retailing industry was becoming increasingly competitive. National chains like Kmart, Target, and Wal-Mart were competing head-to-head with smaller regional chains like Pamida, ShopKo, Ames, and Duckwall-ALCO. The competition forced companies to become more efficient and reduce prices. As we have seen, Wal-Mart and Target have met the challenges while Kmart, Pamida, and others have not. Customers have gained by receiving convenient access to needed products at low prices. Without

63

competition, it is doubtful that consumers would enjoy wide selections at such prices.

Competition also dictates the wage rates in discount retailing and provides a powerful incentive for people to improve their skills and knowledge. It takes very little skill to stock shelves after the customers have gone home. Since most people possess that ability, an abundant supply of labor is available for that job. Wage rates remain low because of this abundant supply of labor. On the other hand, the ability to simultaneously supervise 50 people, manage inventory budgets, and coordinate the operation of a store that generates millions of dollars in sales requires a person with different skills. Because fewer people possess these skills, the wage rate is correspondingly higher.

I learned a lesson about labor competition when I started working for Kmart. At that time I had the notion that I wanted to work in the capital budgeting department at Kmart's international headquarters. Unfortunately for me, I found out that quite a few other people were also interested in the job. To get a job in Kmart's finance department, you had to have a master's degree in finance. I didn't have such a degree, so I didn't get the job. That was a sad experience, but it did teach me the value of continually improving my skills and knowledge. Having a degree would not guarantee my success. However, if I ever hoped to compete successfully against others who wanted the same job, I had better be able to offer more than I at that time possessed. It is this competition for talent that is rewarded by the market. Generally, those who possess skills that are in short supply will get the jobs that pay higher wages.

Economics aside, Scripture also rejects the notion that every person deserves a guaranteed living wage. Proverbs 6:6-11 describes how laziness results in poverty. The apostle Paul in 2 Thessalonians 3:10 says, "If a man will not work, he shall not eat." And even though Paul had a right to expect that the local congregations would support him, he still worked as a tent maker. Christians are not to be lazy and are not to live off the kindness of others. Guaranteeing everyone a wage that conforms to his or her standard of living offers no incentive to work. And because we are all sinners, we do indeed need incentives to work!

God says in the Seventh Commandment, "You shall not steal." Clearly we are not to take what does not belong to us or demand a certain standard of living if we haven't worked for it. One commentator made this observation: "The Bible nowhere says that 'each person,' 'each man,' or 'every head of household' has the right to own private property; it says only that no one may take another's property or goods from him."[14]

Some people criticize labor relations in this country, arguing that employers have greater bargaining power than employees when negotiating labor contracts. The underlying assumption seems to be that since we are stewards of God's creation, a business has a responsibility to help the community with no regard for its own profitability. In addition, because a business can be successful only with the help of its employees, some feel those employees have a right to be involved in the decision-making process within the firm. Specifically, they believe that when a firm plans to close a plant or move a factory, its workers have the right to be involved early on in these decisions.

I believe that business does have a responsibility to help the community. However, neither Scripture nor economic theory states that employees and employers should have equal bargaining power. In fact, the Scriptures assume that distinctions among people will always exist. Our world will always have its slaves, merchants, soldiers, tax collectors, and rulers. Some will possess more material goods than others. Yet we have every reason to be content. Paul tells us in 1 Timothy 6:8, "If we have food and clothing, we will be content with that." The equality the Bible underscores is a spiritual equality. "For we were all baptized by one Spirit into one body—whether Jews or Greeks, slave or free—and we were all given the one Spirit to drink" (1 Corinthians 12:13).

Salvation is free to all people no matter what their stations in life. In our relationship to God, we are all equals. But not necessarily in our relationships to one another. While it is true that employees help create successful businesses, that doesn't give them license to be involved in the daily management of the firm. Paul does not say that slaves deserve to be free. Instead, he tells them, "All who are under the yoke of slavery should consider their masters worthy of full respect, so that God's name and our teaching may not be slandered" (1 Timothy 6:1). From this we can glean that people will have different stations in life, stations which will carry different responsibilites and obligations. The bottom line is that we do not have a "right" to be involved in anything. Our rewards come from the grace of God. If he allows us to be involved in business planning, so be it. If he does not, we are not to complain. It may be nice if employers would involve more employees in the daily decision process. But employers are under no scriptural injunction to do so.

Scripture does give Christians sound principles to follow when engaged in business. It is important that we do not ignore the needs of the poor and less fortunate in society. We should not take advantage of our employees for our own material gain. Focusing on our own material gain and our own individual needs at the expense of the less fortunate is not God pleasing. On the other hand, pursuing material possessions is not, in and of itself, wrong. God expects us to manage his resources wisely. He promises to richly bless our service, which is given in thanks for his grace.

Jonathan Sacks sums up our view of economics in society in the last paragraph of his article "Markets and Morals."

> A great rabbi once taught this lesson to a successful but unhappy businessman. He took him to the window and asked him, "What do you see?" He replied, "I see the world." He then took him to a mirror and asked, "What do you

see?" He replied, "I see myself." "That," said the rabbi, "is what happens when silver covers glass. Instead of seeing the world you see only yourself."

    I agree. It is not the economic system that is at fault but our sinful nature.[15]

SEVEN

BUSINESS ETHICS:
an expression of faith

"But you, man of God, flee from all this, and pursue righteousness, godliness, faith, love, endurance and gentleness."
—Apostle Paul (1 Timothy 6:11)

The previous chapters have demonstrated how economic forces shape the business environment in which Christians and non-Christians compete. How we decide to compete in the market is the focus of this chapter.

Making ethical decisions can be a complicated process for Christians in business, because secular society has divorced ethics from God. A textbook on business ethics defines *ethics* as "the study of what is good for human beings."[1] The same author goes on to observe that ethics and religion are not the same thing. To prove his point, he states, "Certain religious prescriptions have been considered by others to be immoral or unethical, such as religious decrees prohibiting abortion or euthanasia."[2] Without God, ethical decision making is based on the principles of "1) honesty, 2) integrity, 3) promise-keeping, 4) fidelity, 5) fairness, 6) caring for others, 7) respect for others, 8) responsible citizenship, 9) pursuit of excellence, and 10) accountability."[3] By identifying the ethical principle involved, ethical decisions can supposedly be made every time.

While the principles listed are noble, failing to base them on a solid foundation will eventually lead to some type of ethical subjectivism. This theory of ethics is based on the premise that what is ethical for me may not be ethical for you. In other words, determining what is ethical is left up to the individual—no universal truths apply to all people at any given time.

This theory raises some basic problems. For example, what does it mean to care for others? The Netherlands has become the first democratic country to decriminalize euthanasia.[4] Many argue that ending life early in cases where the patient is suffering immense pain is an act of compassion. Others call it murder. The point is that, without a common understanding of the terms, it will be hard to delineate ethical conduct.

Focusing on the horizontal relationship between humans at the expense of the vertical relationship between humans and God fosters ethical subjectivism. As sinful human beings, we have lost the perfect understanding of God's Word. This does not mean that we cannot tell right from wrong in regard to the Fifth Commandment. God is quite clear. "You shall not kill." We may go through all sorts of logical gymnastics to try to justify euthanasia, but nothing changes God's decree that life is his precious gift that only he has the right to take. Only on the bedrock of God's Word do those previously listed principles have substance and meaning. Only when we can measure our temporal behavior by the standard of God's unchanging Word can we get a true reflection of what is ethical.

Society's attitude about what is ethical is often based on material wealth. The last years of President Clinton's presidency provide an example. After seven years of strong economic growth coupled with a growing budget surplus, Americans were feeling confident about the future. With low unemployment and even lower inflation rates, the moral indiscretions of the president were shrugged off as partisan politics. Even the disturbing trend in which corporations announced record profits one day and then laid off thousands of employees the next failed to arouse public sentiment.[5] Apparently, a rising stock market can placate the soccer moms of society. However, while Americans may be quite willing to exchange moral values for economic growth, the apostle Paul was not. Speaking to the cosmopolitan and economically successful Corinthians, Paul warned them about abandoning their faith in favor of a popular social culture. Americans, including Christian business leaders, can learn from his message.

The people in the young Corinthian congregation that the apostle Paul had established faced the challenge of turning from the ways of society and walking according to their faith in Christ. Remember that Corinth, situated on a major east/west trade route, was a pluralistic society composed of people from many different cultures and religions. If the congregation looked anything like the general population, the membership included plenty of people with differing opinions and from differing cultural perspectives. While they may have been united in one faith, they were just learning how to express that faith. Without a complete Bible or the benefit of years of spiritual growth, they often stumbled. Paul, the expert they had looked to for guidance, had moved on to continue his work. Without him to guide them, they quickly reverted to the ways of their society. And their society condoned lax moral attitudes, championed a Hellenistic philosophy that emphasized the importance of a person's ability, and worshiped a variety of idols. In addition to this, the Corinthians had to deal with a well-established Jewish population that saw the upstart Christians as a threat to their religion. The pressure to conform to the status quo that the early Christians must have felt cannot be understated.

Given this backdrop, Paul's message to the Corinthians (1 Corinthians 10:1-10) provides today's Christian businesspersons with a useful context in which to see their lives and business practices. In their lives, the Israelites had failed to exercise self-discipline. In the same way, the proud Corinthians made a habit of pushing the boundaries, even to the point of returning to their idol worship. Israel's history would provide a powerful warning against betraying the Lord in this way. In the first four verses, Paul compared the Israelites' deliverance from Egypt to our baptisms. The Israelites had been saved by water as they passed through the Red Sea. As they passed through the waters, they were bound to Moses, their leader sent from God.

Verse 5 was of special interest to the Corinthian Christians. Paul warned the Corinthians about the danger of losing their salvation, even though they considered themselves Christians. "Nevertheless, God was not pleased with most of them; their bodies were scattered over the desert." The Corinthians thought that because they had been given freedom through the gospel, this was carte blanche to go out and sin. Paul expressly rejected this notion when he wrote that such conduct in the past had led to the destruction of a large number of God's chosen people.

This lesson remains relevant today. We too live in a society that places a great deal of emphasis on freedom, intellect, and commerce. Essentially, many in our society have made these their idols that they now worship instead of God. For example, instead of worrying about sexual immorality, the city of Milwaukee has established a gay registry, so homosexual couples can ostensibly establish stable relationships.[6] We are so "enlightened" that what God has to say about the subject is irrelevant. Anyone who disagrees with the politically correct view is considered intellectually dormant. But our perspective is entirely different from the world's, because we are bound to Christ. Through our baptisms we have been set apart from the world.

These words give much food for thought for business leaders. Our love affair with the stock market lays bare for all to see the lust this society has for money. Our market economy has no compassion for anything that might hurt profits. The demand for increasingly higher returns forces management to squeeze economic resources, including labor, so that profits will justify those expectations. Therefore, we see companies earning record profits and paying handsome salaries to CEOs, but firing employees.[7] Labor, like a lump of coal, has become just another production variable that needs to be factored in in order to maximize profits. Christian businesspeople are pressured to jump on society's bandwagon. Economic efficiency aside, this is no way to treat God's prized creation.

In 1 Corinthians 10:6-10, Paul pointed to the fall of Israel to encourage the Corinthians to avoid the temptations of a godless society. Corinthians found it especially easy to talk the talk but far more difficult to walk the walk. They were used to drinking, partying, and engaging in immoral behavior. Paul warned them that God does not tolerate such behavior, especially from his chosen people.

Christian business leaders need to recognize that we place ourselves in serious spiritual danger when we adopt the ways of unbelieving businesspeople. "Getting along by going along" cannot be our motto. How many times have we heard about businesspeople going to exotic nightclubs to entertain clients, because they felt it was necessary if they were to land the account? Such conduct hardly glorifies God's holy name. Or how many times have American businesses complained about government interference in private matters because OSHA imposed a new safety rule? How many times have they tried to circumvent the rules? If the crane disaster at Milwaukee's Miller Park was actually the result of management pressure to meet deadlines at all costs, then we can appreciate the role of the government, which God created to preserve order and safety.

If we try to invoke the everyone-else-does-it excuse, Paul takes away our excuse. "No temptation has seized you except what is common to man. And God is faithful; he will not let you be tempted beyond what you can bear. But when you are tempted, he will also provide a way out so that you can stand up under it" (1 Corinthians 10:13). The work the Holy Spirit began with our baptisms continues. Having set us apart for God, the Holy Spirit provides ways for us to stand up under temptation. When faced with difficult choices, we turn to him. He shows us how we are able to glorify God in our business dealings. He can give us the courage to do what is right.

The gospel message found in Luke 16:1-9 adds an additional important encouragement that businesspeople can apply to their lives. In the parable, Jesus told of the shrewd manager who was about to be fired by his employer. Before that fateful day arrived, the manager reduced the amount that his employer's creditors owed, thus ensuring that when he was without a job, they would help him out. Jesus used the man as an example not that we should emulate his dishonesty, but that we should creatively use our gifts, talents, and opportunities to win converts for our Savior. That, finally, is the goal of every Christian, also the Christian businessperson.

American business leaders are too quick to defend sinful business practices, hiding behind the excuse that this is the way it is done in business. The implication for us is that if we act like Christians, we may end up in bankruptcy court. The sport-utility vehicles, three-week vacations, and large homes give us very comfortable lifestyles. The thought of sacrificing all of this may weaken our resolve. Paul didn't let the ancient Corinthians get away with this reasoning. It doesn't hold for us either. Living for Christ can affect us economically. But our security is not found at the bottom line of our bank statement. Our security rests in God's signature attached to his wonderful promises to be with us and to provide for us.

A Christian businessperson would do well to regularly reread the Old Testament account of the life of Joseph. Begin with the story of Joseph and Potiphar's wife in Genesis 39. Betrayed by his brothers, Joseph was taken into slavery in Egypt. But God was with Joseph, and Joseph was soon in charge of Potiphar's entire estate. When Potiphar's wife tried to seduce Joseph, he resisted. His sinful nature could have devised several reasons for him to bow to her wishes. Besides feeding his own desires, he might have seen an opportunity to advance his own career. Choosing instead to honor God, Joseph ended up facing a long prison term. But even though his life seemed to continue on a downward spiral, Joseph did not doubt God. Years later he saw clearly that God had used all these challenging events to bless him and the rest of God's people. With all the career counseling in the world, Joseph could not have planned this path.

The lesson taken from the story of Joseph for those in business is that God does not abandon his people. Standing up for Christ may have negative implications. It is possible that our businesses could suffer—we could lose very important contracts or could be fired from good jobs. However, Paul's observation is our comfort: "We know that in all things God works for the good of those who love him, who have been called according to his purpose" (Romans 8:28). Those who are "called" receive that call via the work of the Holy Spirit through the Word and sacrament. Our success need not be the focus of our lives. Our focus is, and always must remain, on the cross, where we find our highest treasure. In fact, if we focus on anything else, we are clearly wasting our lives.

Jesus once told a parable about a fig tree that for three years didn't bear fruit (Luke 13:6-8). Only the gardener's urgent pleas on behalf of the tree spared it from the ax. He promised that for one more year he would give the tree the finest care. Then, if no fruit were found, he would cut the tree down. I sometimes wonder if, by the way we conduct business, we don't look a little like that fig tree that bears no fruit. Are we so entrenched in the ways of the sinful world that we fail to bear fruit for God? Are we in business to make as much money as we can for ourselves only? Do we use God's natural resources with no concern for how it affects his creation? If so, how long will the Lord tolerate our sinful actions?

If we doubt that we can be good businesspersons and Christians at the same time, we might find encouragement in the call of Moses (Exodus 3:1-15). Moses had major reservations about doing what God wanted. However, the Lord reassured Moses that he would be with him and would give him the words and strength to carry out his work. Like Moses, we find it expedient to claim incompetence when it comes to carrying out the work of the Lord. It is far easier to go about our business the way society expects rather than to make waves and stick out in the crowd. Of course, Moses was incompetent. So are we. But over time Moses realized that his success did not depend upon his own wit or eloquence or leadership abilities. By the time the Israelites were ready to leave Sinai, Moses knew that they would succeed only if God were with them.

"Moses said to him, 'If your Presence does not go with us, do not send us up from here'" (33:15). It won't be our business savvy or our ability to manage people or our understanding of the markets that will spawn our success. Every good gift is from above. Like Moses and the Israelites, we too can succeed only if God is with us.

It was for good reason that the apostle Paul used Moses and the Israelites as warnings for God's New Testament people. To turn from God is to make a fatal mistake.

These words remind us all of our need for a Savior in the times when we remove God's will from our business plans. They remind us that we cannot save ourselves. How thankful we can be that God's words do not stop there but go on to tell us of the Savior's work on our behalf to remove our guilt. Because of his death and resurrection, we know we have a higher goal than stockpiling earthly wealth. And we know that God is with us always.

During my years in retailing, Christmas took on a new meaning. Gone were the days of wondrous excitement as I waited with eager anticipation for the day to arrive. Retail work turned the holiday season into a purely commercial exercise. The long hours, hard work, and frayed nerves of employees and customers alike made it hard for me to enjoy the season. Others also lamented that the holiday season had lost all meaning. As a Christian businessman, that presented me with an ethical dilemma. At some point during the holiday season, I would hear, in a sermon, how Christ's birthday was being commercialized. What I longed to hear was just what we as Christians were supposed to do about that. As a Christian and manager of a discount retail store, how much responsibility did I have to accept for the commercialization of Christmas? Most of my store's profits were earned during the Christmas selling season. We started early, stayed open late, and pushed for every dollar that we could make. As a Christian, how do you balance the ethical pursuit of profit with the knowledge that you are contributing to the degradation of the Lord's birthday? This is just one example of the countless ethical dilemmas with which Christians must struggle.

Or try this one on for size. You are the chief executive officer of a large paint manufacturer. Before 1940, your company sold paint that contained lead. You now know that lead is harmful to human health. You also know that small children who ingest lead can become sick. One day you receive a request from the Milwaukee Common Council asking your company to remove the lead paint from all the older homes in the city. The cost of such a project would run in the millions of dollars. As a Christian and a CEO, just what is your responsibility to the city and your God?

Finally, look at an example of something that actually happened in the tire industry several years ago. Firestone Tire and Rubber Company recalled a line of tires after it became known that the failure of these tires had caused a number of deaths. But if you were the president of Firestone, how would you have known when it was time to actually order a recall? We now know that over 80 deaths were linked to the failure of the tires. Firestone has been criticized for not moving fast enough on the recall. As a Christian, how do you make the recall decision? How many people have to die before you act? One person? Ten people? Twenty people? How do you know?

The frustrating thing for Christians is that these questions are not necessarily any easier for us to answer than for unbelievers. We might even argue that the questions are more difficult for us. Why? As a Christian I not only have to please investors, consumers, and the government, but I am compelled by love to glorify God and serve my fellow people.

If I turn to my Concordia Self-Study Bible and look up tire recalls, retailing, or lead paint, I will not find answers. There are no specific passages that deal with these issues. How can I ever be sure that my answer to any one of these questions will be God pleasing?

May I suggest we start by looking at Psalm 51:5, "Surely I was sinful at birth, sinful from the time my mother conceived me?" From the cutest infant to the crustiest of adults, we have all sinned and earned eternal damnation. There is nothing we can do on our own to please our God or save ourselves. Though for centuries we have focused our best philosophical reasoning skills on the question of how we can attain eternal life on our own, we have failed to find the way. There is none. If our flawed human reason is unable to design a satisfactory plan for our salvation, what hope is there that we can ever find a fulfilling answer to a tire recall, a lead paint removal problem, or too much commercialism?

How thankful we can be that we have a gracious and loving God. For a reason I can't really begin to understand, God has given us a way out. He not only sent us a Savior, but he also gave us the faith to believe in that Savior. Through the Sacrament of Holy Baptism, he conquered our rebellious hearts and changed our lives. Paul wrote about that change, "Consequently, you are no longer foreigners and aliens, but fellow citizens with God's people and members of God's household" (Ephesians 2:19).

Think about the implications of our baptisms. As Christians, we are not alone playing a zero-sum game that we are destined to lose. Our merciful and gracious God is with us every step of the way, inviting us to trust in him, assuring us through his apostle that "I am convinced that neither death nor life, neither angels nor demons, neither the present nor the future, nor any powers, neither height nor depth, nor anything else in all creation, will be able to separate us from the love of God that is in Christ Jesus, our Lord" (Romans 8:38,39).

Baptism stands as a powerful example that demonstrates the love that God has for all people. The changes God has worked in us through our baptisms form the context of the decisions we make as Christian businesspeople. How do I put my faith into action? The answer involves more than simply looking up a one-size-fits-all Bible passage. Ethical decisions flow from our understanding of what it means to be members of God's family—children of God. As heirs of the treasures of heaven, we want our entire lives to reflect the words of Paul: "Whatever you do, whether in word or deed, do it all in the name of the Lord Jesus, giving thanks to God the Father through him" (Colossians 3:17). We trust that God, who works saving faith in us through the Holy Spirit, will also work in our hearts so that our lives and actions might give all glory to him.

The more we focus on what God has done for us, the more we are strengthened in the conviction that Christians don't have to check their faith at the office door. Whether it is Joseph, Moses, or any of the other numerous examples recorded in the Bible, it is unmistakable that God guides, protects, and blesses those who believe in him.

EIGHT

PROFITS: ETHICS, money, and business

"The worst crime against working people is a company which fails to operate at a profit."—*Samuel Gompers*

Economics is the study of how society allocates scarce resources in order to satisfy the unlimited material wants of the people. Business addresses how those goods and services are profitably produced. The fact that money is involved doesn't insinuate that business in and of itself is evil. Money is not evil, nor is it evil to possess money. When money becomes more important than God, then our attitude about money has become evil and we easily succumb to evil desires.

As is true in other areas of our lives, our motive is key. It would be a mistake to suppose that we could use our business talents to somehow establish a good relationship with God— or to earn our salvation. The Bible is brimming with stories of economically successful people who fell woefully short in the eyes of God. The rich young man mentioned in Matthew 19 comes immediately to mind. He imagined that he had kept God's commandments. But Jesus directed him to consider his attitude toward his wealth in order to show the young man that he hadn't kept even the First Commandment. After the man walked away moping, Jesus proclaimed a sober truth: "Again I tell you, it is easier for a camel to go through the eye of a needle than for a rich man to enter the kingdom of God" (verse 24). Wealth brings its own set of temptations. But we don't use it simply to promote our own earthly comfort to earn God's favor. We use the blessings God has given us to glorify him.

Christian businesspersons daily walk the fine line between pursuing profit in a God-pleasing way and becoming trapped by, what Luther would term, "damnable greed." It is too easy for critics to accuse businesses of making too much money. When gasoline prices surged during the summer of 2000, even the government launched an investigation into whether the oil companies were ripping off consumers. Vice President Al Gore was quick to attack "big oil," saying that the oil companies were using the shortage to pad their bottom line. But what is "too much"? John D. Rockefeller was reportedly asked how much money would be enough. He replied, "Just a little bit more." Martin Luther was no more explicit. In his treatise *Trade and Usury,* Luther said merchants should "seek in your mind an adequate living." I suspect that Luther's definition of "adequate living" was quite different than Rockefeller's. The problem remains the same—when have we made enough profit?

Before tackling that issue, we need to define what is meant by *profit*. In his article *Profits: Some Moral Reflections*, author Paul F. Camenisch explains how difficult it is to define the term adequately. If we consider *profit* to be "the difference between total receipts and total expenses," the obvious question is whether the amount of the difference, the profit, can be justified. Why does the business need to earn that much money if it has already paid all the bills? The argument changes a bit if you define *profit* as "the reward for taking risk." But, inevitably, someone will ask whether the risk to be taken justifies the amount of the reward.[1] The question is not about whether you can justify making a profit. The question is, Just how much is enough?

From an economic standpoint, businesses are the agents that the economic system uses to provide consumers with the goods and services they demand. Remember that through the economic system, choices are made about what goods will be produced, for whom they will be produced, and how they will be produced. It is the business that takes these choices and transforms them into actual products and services. In this way, business fulfills a vital role within our economic system. It just so happens that in fulfilling that role, firms earn a profit. Within a market economy, profit is a natural part of the system.

Earning a profit can also be justified scripturally. Under inspiration of God, Solomon wrote, "All hard work brings a profit, but mere talk leads only to poverty" (Proverbs 14:23). The apostle Paul wrote, "Who serves as a soldier at his own expense? Who plants a vineyard and does not eat of its grapes? Who tends a flock and does not drink of the milk?" (1 Corinthians 9:7). We have a right to expect that our labor will produce incomes for us. As we have seen before, God expects us to work his creation for his glory and our benefit. Pursued with a proper attitude and reaped in a God-pleasing way, profit can be viewed as a gift from God.

Christians need not be ashamed of earning a profit from legitimate business activities. However, business in general needs to become more involved in the debate about how much profit is justified. In this debate, Christian business leaders will play a vital role. Our stand will reflect our goal to glorify God. All of our work and business activities will be in tune with the business ethic Paul proposed: "Whatever you do, work at it with all your heart, as working for the Lord, not for men" (Colossians 3:23). When Christians engage in business activities that are God pleasing, the profit issue goes away. Granted, in a sinful world there will always be critics who accuse businesses of making too much money. Our purpose is not to mollify sinful unbelievers. Our task is to honor our God.

So, for a Christian, conducting business always involves more than just making money. Our business practices express our attitudes toward society, human relationships, and God. A study of business ethics helps us see whether our behavior is moral or immoral. For sinful people, herein lies the rub. Who determines what is moral?

A recent survey of Amazon.com, a large online book retailer, found over 13,000 books dealing with ethics.[2] It appears that telling right from wrong has become a big business and that there is no shortage of experts on the subject.

Contemporary business ethics focuses on the importance of corporate social responsibility, or the idea that business must be sensitive to the environment in which it operates.[3] Historically, this meant that corporations had an obligation to their primary stakeholders. These stakeholders included investors, employees, customers, and suppliers. Businesses met their ethical obligations by maximizing profits while operating within the law. Robert Eaton, former CEO of Chrysler Corporation, explained, "Companies that focus on making money become more competitive, and that in turn means more economic growth, and more jobs, and all the other things that 'stakeholders' care about."[4] In practice, such ethical behavior constitutes activities that are lawful and that increase the return for those who are directly affected.[5] As the old saying goes, "What is good for GM [or should we say Chrysler] is good for America."

The idea of corporate social responsibility can be traced back to the 1920s. It is based on the notion of a "social contract" between a business and society. Stakeholders expected the corporation to do the right thing. Two principles form the underpinning of the social contract: the charity principle and the stewardship principle.[6]

The charity principle reflected the idea that business should help the needy. Following this principle, Andrew Carnegie had given away $322 million by 1913 and John D. Rockefeller had donated approximately $175 million to the needy. We have also seen expressions of that principle in more recent times, for example, in Ted Turner's $100-million gift to the United Nations.

The stewardship principle is based on the premise that businesses are public trustees of the earth's resources and should consider the interests of all who are affected by their decisions. Managers are stewards of the resources entrusted to them. Businesspeople have an obligation to all of society.

As corporations become larger, many people believe that corporations have a greater responsibility for the well-being of society. Consider that statement in the context of the following statistics: If we were to rank the world's one hundred largest economies, fifty would belong to corporations.[7] Yearly sales for

GM[8] are about four times the size of the Wisconsin State budget.[9] Although the world's largest industrial corporations employ only .005 of 1 percent of the world's population, these companies control 25 percent of the world's economic output. The top three hundred transnational corporations control 25 percent of the world's productive assets.[10] The concentration of economic power in the hands of corporations has some suggesting that businesses should also be responsible to secondary stakeholders like local communities and governments.[11] They reason that corporations have an obligation to give something back to the communities in which they conduct business.

Not everyone believes that corporations actually have a social responsibility. Milton Friedman, a Nobel prize-winning economist, argued strongly against the idea. In an article titled *The Social Responsibility of Business Is to Increase Its Profits,* Friedman argued, "Only people can have responsibilities. A corporation is an artificial person and in this sense may have artificial responsibilities, but 'business' as a whole cannot be said to have responsibilities, even in this vague sense."[12] His point was that individuals can spend their money however they want. In a corporation, shareholders hire managers to protect and promote the shareholders' interests. Presumably, this means increasing the shareholders' returns. Unless a majority of the shareholders condones the socially responsible activity, it could be considered stealing. As agents of the corporation, managers must do everything to protect their owners' interests.

Friedman's viewpoint has historical support. In 1916 John and Horace Dodge sued Henry Ford, because Ford refused to pay them a stock dividend. Instead, Ford had cut the price of his automobiles from $440 to $360 per car. It seems that Henry Ford believed his company was too profitable and that some of the wealth could be shared with the general public by reducing the price of his cars. The Dodge brothers argued that Ford's primary responsibility was to his shareholders. Since Ford planned to pay only $1.2 million in dividends and to reinvest into the business the remaining profit of $58 million, the Dodges felt they were being cheated. The court agreed with the Dodge brothers and ordered Ford to pay the dividends.[13]

A problem with the concept of social responsibility is that it presents a moving target for business executives. People tend to interpret each social contract in the context of the economic and social conditions of the day. Pabst Brewing Company became embroiled in a nasty lawsuit over health benefits when the company unilaterally tried to stop paying health insurance premiums for its retired workers. Stiffer competition in the beer market was forcing Pabst to cut costs. In less-competitive times, Pabst might not even have considered cutting costs at the expense of its retired workers.

The ethical principles of the general public also change. Kohl's Department Stores have found that selling jeans made by peasants in Nicaragua creates ill will in the United States.[14] Student protests are forcing colleges and universities to review the labor practices of vendors who provide college apparel. Students are demanding that working conditions in factories that make college apparel be improved.[15]

Globalization has made the issue of social responsibility even more complex by forcing American companies to review the way business is conducted overseas. Some question whether it is ethical to do business in China when we know its government persecutes Christians and imprisons critics. Others wonder if corporations are upholding their responsibilities to their communities when they shift production to other countries in order to save on labor costs.

Environmental concerns and technological changes also have made the business landscape more complex. We want businesses to be God-pleasing stewards of the earth's resources. Global warming is possibly altering our environment. Rain forests are being decimated at an alarming rate. Ecologically sensitive lands are being used for development. As many as half of all known plant and animal species are headed toward extinction within the next one hundred years.[16] Business practices that contribute to these problems are hard to justify as good stewardship.

Businesses also have to wrestle with the question of how to balance the need to protect employee and customer privacy with the need to offer more goods and services. My local grocery store uses a preferred-customer card to offer discounts on purchases I make at the store. Its goal is to build a database so the store can tailor promotions to each individual customer. Do we really want corporations keeping track of what we buy? Do we want marketers accessing and sharing this information with others? Advances in technology have made DNA research possible. It may soon be possible to determine if employees are predisposed to certain kinds of occupational injuries, workplace violence, or more. Should businesses be allowed to make employment decisions based on this type of information?

The point is that social responsibility does not provide Christians with a useful guideline for conducting business. Standards change and sinful humans are biased toward their own self-interests. Christians don't want to follow the pattern of the world. "Do not conform any longer to the pattern of this world, but be transformed by the renewing of your mind. Then you will be able to test and approve what God's will is—his good, pleasing and perfect will" (Romans 12:2). Instead of looking to society for an answer, Christians turn to God, asking for the courage and the wisdom to apply the love of Christ to our business dealings. God has given us his ethical guidelines in the form of the Ten Commandments. The requirement of God's law is that we demonstrate love toward our God and our fellow people. Christ gave a succinct explanation of what God expects from us when he said, "Love the Lord your God with all your heart and with all your soul and with all your mind and with all your strength," and "Love your neighbor as yourself" (Mark 12:30,31). Those are the greatest commandments, but by themselves, they don't give us motivation or courage to follow ethical business practices. That motivation and courage we can find only in what Christ has done for us. He came to earth—for us. He kept God's law perfectly—for us. He died—for us. He has revealed that our greatest treasure is the eternal life that he has won for us. As recipients of this great treasure, our response is to glorify God in all we do and in our dealings with others: "A new command I give you: Love one another. As I have loved you, so you must love one another. By this all men will know that you are my disciples, if you love one another" (John 13:34,35). The law serves as a guide to show us which works please God. We recognize that the psalmist's words are true: "Your word is a lamp to my feet and a light for my path" (Psalm 119:105).

Christians in business are sometimes frustrated by the fact that in the secular marketplace, making ethical decisions may be no easier for us than it is for unbelievers. Christians face the same fast-paced and unforgiving market that unbelievers face. But Christians are more likely to struggle with an additional concern: the well-being of other human beings. For example, currency markets handle over $1 trillion per day.[17] Traders buy and sell a country's currency as if it were a bushel of corn. When a currency loses value, traders move to more attractive investments. A massive outflow of money by currency traders can result in an economic downturn for a local economy. You may recall the example of the 1997–98 Asian financial crisis.[18] The economies of many Pacific-rim countries were thrown into turmoil, which resulted in the loss of jobs and a reduced standard of living for thousands of people. The problem is that the people who make the decisions that impact a local economy may be thousands of miles away and never see or feel the ramifications. Their focus is on profits and not on how their decisions will affect the local population.

In our capitalist economic system, such economic disruptions are accepted as necessary evils in the quest to increase overall economic growth. But for the Christian, that trade-off can't be justified quite so easily. We know that Christ's command "Love your neighbor as yourself" applies also to the economic marketplace. It applies to the decision to move production facilities to Mexico and to the decision to buy clothes from Nicaragua. For us to hide behind excuses, such as "This is business," would be an outright lie.

But the questions will not always be easy to answer. The Bible doesn't speak directly about such issues as corporate downsizing, CEO compensation, or outsourcing. However, we have the assurance that we can take every problem to God in prayer. We can ask God to remove all selfish motivation from our hearts and to fill us with the firm resolve that our every decision will reflect the love of Christ shown to us on the cross. We know that in the pages of God's Word we will find help to recognize the principles that apply and the promise that he will walk beside us.

We desperately need those words of guidance and promise, especially when we are under pressure to make a profit.

A controversy involving Sunbeam and the accounting firm of Arthur Andersen demonstrates just how overwhelming that pressure can be. In the pursuit of profit, managers of both firms ignored ethical norms. The results were devastating.

Al Dunlap was the chairman of Sunbeam at the time. The maker of kitchen appliances was floundering. Dunlap's job was to put the company back on its feet. Known as "Chainsaw Al," Dunlap had a reputation for saving failing companies. He was a flamboyant, bombastic chief executive who was willing to do whatever needed to be done to deliver the profits. Cutting costs was his favorite approach, especially terminating employees.

Though business schools will focus on Dunlap's strategic management skills, they should evaluate the ethics of his decisions and practices. On May 15, 2001, the Securities and Exchange Commission (SEC) announced that it was charging "Chainsaw Al" with fraud. According to the SEC, Sunbeam inflated its profits by fictitiously selling spare parts to another firm. The ruse went like this: Sunbeam sold its inventory of repair parts to another firm for $11 million. One estimate put the actual value of the spare parts as low as $2 million. Whatever the actual value, the sale allowed Sunbeam to post an $8 million profit. After posting the year-end profits, Sunbeam bought back the spare parts. According to the SEC, the profits were really the result of creative and fraudulent bookkeeping.[19]

Though Dunlap's manipulation of the accounting system was bad enough, the story didn't end there. It appears that the auditing firm hired to verify the books perpetuated Dunlap's scam. The firm, Arthur Andersen, was one of the largest public accounting firms in America. When auditors for Andersen questioned the legitimacy of the spare-parts transaction, Sunbeam agreed to reduce the reported profit by $3 million. Arthur Andersen accepted the compromise and signed off on the books.

Independent audits of public firms are intended to provide a degree of assurance that the financial statements prepared by management are accurate. The auditor's report is part of every annual report produced by a publicly traded firm. It is probably safe to say that most investors have never read the auditor's report. The report, usually in the form of a letter, will usually contain language similar to that found in AG Edwards' 2001 annual report: "We conducted our audits in accordance with auditing standards generally accepted in the United States of America. Those standards require that we plan and perform the audit to obtain reasonable assurance about whether the financial statements are free of material misstatement. An audit includes examining, on a test basis, evidence supporting the amounts and disclosures in the financial statements. An audit also includes assessing the accounting principles used and significant estimates made by management, as well as evaluating the overall financial statement presentation. We believe that our audits provide a reasonable basis for our opinion."[20] For investors, the fact that the financial reports "present fairly, in all material respects, the financial position" of the company gives them a basis upon which to make intelligent investment decisions.

While the audit report is not all that interesting, the case of Sunbeam underscores its importance. The SEC maintains that the $11 million profit listed in the financial statements was outside the scope of generally accepted accounting rules. However, when Sunbeam refused to lower the profit by more than $3 million, the independent auditors caved. Arthur Andersen Accounting reclassified the profit as immaterial.

Since it was no longer material, Arthur Andersen Accounting could say that the financial statements fairly represented, "in all material respects," the financial position of the company.[21] In effect, the independent auditors helped Sunbeam fool investors by making a phony profit look legitimate.

Our desire to let our lights shine means that profits do not become our exclusive priority. It is easy to see how the pursuit of profit in a sinful world could blur our decision making. Henry Ford and Al Dunlap are examples demonstrating the pressure to make money in a market economy. Focusing primarily on profit can cause us to forget about the people who will be affected. Laying off people and moving a plant to Mexico is not, in and of itself, wrong. Whether we like it or not, Master Lock had sound economic reasons for moving. As Christians, though, it should cause us to think twice if our motivation for moving the plant is simply to increase profits so the financial analysts are impressed.

NINE

LUTHER
and capitalism

"A Christian man is the most free lord of all, and subject to none; a Christian man is the most dutiful servant of all, and subject to every one."—*Martin Luther (Concerning Christian Liberty, 1520)*

I suspect that most American Christians take for granted the fact that they live and work in a market economy. I also believe that Martin Luther would be surprised, and possibly dismayed, by our attitude toward capitalism. To be sure, Martin Luther did not understand market economic theory. (It developed two hundred years after he lived.) While his insights and concerns were not based on strong theoretical principles, they are no less insightful or relevant today. By examining Luther's 1524 treatise *Trade and Usury*, we can more fully appreciate how susceptible market economies are to sinful behavior. We will focus especially on three areas: pricing, lending, and the role of government in the market.

Because the blessing of the Reformation stemmed from a struggle to reclaim the gospel, Christians easily forget the economic changes that were taking place during Luther's lifetime. Up to that time, feudalism dominated the economic landscape. Controlled by the lord of the manor, feudal estates were really mini states. Instead of a national economy, localized feudal economies reigned in any given area. The people who lived on these estates produced goods that sustained the feudal community. In return, the lord of the estate provided each member with a portion of what the community produced. What we would recognize as supply and demand was not the driving force in the feudal economy. But even as Christians were witnessing changes within the church, society was wrestling with changes in economic conditions.

The Reformation took place during the Age of Discovery. North America, South America, and a water route to the Far East were relatively new discoveries. These discoveries had an enormous impact on both the local European economies and the international economic system. Newly discovered lands and trade routes made commerce with other nations possible on a grand scale. These new lands were sources of natural resources that provided some nations with material wealth not previously known. An abundance of gold and silver made commercial transactions easier. People began to move from the countryside to cities, where they specialized in certain crafts and traded for what they could not produce. New products and services filled the marketplace. The increasing mobility of people and goods spelled the end of the feudal system and introduced the market economy.

The trouble with transitions is that they are not necessarily smooth, easy to understand, or eagerly embraced. Luther struggled with the transition. He could see how the change from feudalism to a nascent market system benefited some while it hurt others. What he saw did not please him and certainly influenced his flawed understanding of economic theory. However, the conclusions he reached about balancing a Christ-centered view of our existence with the conflicting demands of an emerging market economy are still very relevant today.

When Martin Luther looked at the market, he did not see an economic system that was efficiently allocating scarce resources based on price. To the contrary, Luther saw unadulterated greed that drove merchants to "sell my goods as dear as I can."[1] A current translation would be to "charge whatever the market can bear." As far as Luther was concerned, merchants who extracted the highest possible price for their wares were doing nothing more than stealing from their neighbors. The desire to maximize profits was less a result of market forces and more an example of materialism and selfishness.

According to Luther, pricing was not something that should be set by the forces of supply and demand. It did not matter whether it was possible to sell a product or service for a higher price. A Christian should set his or her profit by "computing the amount of time and labor you have put into it; and comparing that with the effort of a day laborer who works at some other occupation and seeing how much he earns in a day. On that basis, figure how many days you have spent in getting your wares and bringing them to your place of business, and how much labor and risk was involved; for a great amount of labor and time ought to have a correspondingly greater return."[2] Merchants would earn only what they needed to cover their costs and earn a "reasonable" profit. Anything more Luther considered morally wrong.

Of course, Luther's solution was not necessarily based on sound economic theory. Notice how he ignored the productivity of labor and failed to address whether the products being produced had equal consumer demand. Nowhere did he address the issues of scarcity, quality, and innovation. The need to be compensated for risk seemed to be confused with the concept of time. According to Luther's egalitarian and Christian community-based worldview, the profit motive is a metaphor for sinful behavior, which makes trade nothing more than a socially acceptable form of "robbery and stealing."[3]

Setting aside Luther's naive assumptions about how an economic system should function does not detract from the basic point he was trying to make. Economic activity, while a necessary evil, is never the focal point of Christian thinking. Luther's words offer a pointed reminder: Modern Christian business leaders need to question the necessity of the profit maximization rule that governs our economic and business philosophies. With its mathematical formulas, economic theory may be able to pinpoint the optimal profit maximizing output. But it fails to acknowledge that each of us has been bought and paid for with the blood of Christ. By ignoring the humbling reality of Christ's death, sinful and arrogant humans turn to their own devices to get ahead. Luther wanted to make sure we never forget the implications of Christ's passion, even when we are engaged in business transactions.

To reinforce his point, Luther challenged the common practice of lending. Surety and lending remain common business practices today. However, in 1524 Luther condemned the practices. Surety is an important contractual arrangement whereby one party becomes responsible for the debt of another. If a debtor fails to pay his or her debt when due, the surety must make the payment. A car loan is a practical modern example. Parents who cosign a loan agreement so their 18-year-old son can purchase a car enter into a surety relationship. Lending, of course, usually involves repaying borrowed money with interest. In our modern economic system, these two innovations have become very important tools for achieving economic efficiency. How many of us could buy a car, a home, or a college education if we could not borrow the money?

Luther had a major problem with the surety relationship. He cited Proverbs 20:16; 22:26; and 27:13 as evidence that such arrangements are forbidden by God. It appears that Luther saw the surety relationship as one in which the debtor places his trust in the surety and not in God. To avoid this temptation, Luther encouraged people to only pay cash for the items that they needed. If they could not afford the item, Luther felt they should try to get someone to lend the item to them. And Luther was very clear about the lending relationship. He believed that Christians should lend out of a sense of love and compassion for their neighbors and not because they want to make a quick dollar. "Borrowing would be a fine thing if it were practiced between Christians, for every borrower would then willingly return what had been lent him, and the lender would willingly forgo repayment if the borrower were unable to pay."[4]

According to Luther, the German practice of charging interest on a loan was nothing more than a "slippery and newly invented business [that] very frequently makes itself an upright and loyal protector of damnable greed and usury."[5] He felt that the practice of lending for profit was sinful. From an economic perspective, we do find that the practice is economically inefficient. Instead of investing in projects that result in new goods and services, people might be blinded by the chance of making easy money through lending.

Luther's definition of lending is quite different from our modern understanding of the term. He wrote, "He who makes a charge for lending is not lending, and neither is he selling; therefore, this must be usury, because lending is, in its very nature, nothing else than to offer another something without charge, on the condition that one eventually get back the same thing or its equivalent, and nothing more."⁶ Luther believed that since Christians understood that lending meant giving without the expectation of additional repayment, any type of charge disqualified the act from being a loan.

Christ's words in Matthew 5:384-8 form the basis for Luther's understanding of lending and usury. Christ said,

> You have heard that it was said, "Eye for eye, and tooth for tooth." But I tell you, Do not resist an evil person. If someone strikes you on the right cheek, turn to him the other also. And if someone wants to sue you and take your tunic, let him have your cloak as well. If someone forces you to go one mile, go with him two miles. Give to the one who asks you, and do not turn away from the one who wants to borrow from you. You have heard that it was said, "Love your neighbor and hate your enemy." But I tell you: Love your enemies and pray for those who persecute you, that you may be sons of your Father in heaven. . . . If you love those who love you, what reward will you get? Are not even the tax collectors doing that? And if you greet only your brothers, what are you doing more than others? Do not even pagans do that? Be perfect, therefore, as your heavenly Father is perfect.

Christians do not charge for their love and mercy. They give it freely. Lending and surety corrupt our motivation. Instead of wanting to help our neighbors, we want to get what is theirs by charging for what we should freely give. Simply put, lending is motivated by greed.

Luther's objection to commercial transactions, even those that did not involve lending, is based on his view of Christian love. Paul wrote in 1 Corinthians 13:4,5, "Love is patient, love is kind. It does not envy, it does not boast, it is not proud. It is not rude, it is not self-seeking, it is not easily angered, it keeps no record of wrongs." Luther was convinced that in business transactions, self-interested buyers and sellers were anything but motivated by love or concern for the well-being of others. He made this point quite clear when he wrote, "It may be assumed that with his purchase the buyer is seldom if ever seeking and desiring the welfare and advantage of his neighbor—the seller—as much as or more than his own."[7] The inescapable conclusion for Luther was that market exchanges drove a wedge between Christians and eroded Christian compassion. Further, it replaced Christ with self-love and a desire for temporal goods as the centers of our lives.

Usury is usually defined as the charging of an exorbitant rate of interest on a loan. Part of Luther's hatred of what he termed usury can be traced to the devastating effects the charging of interest was having on his society. Luther clearly believed that the rich were using lending for no other purpose than to increase their own incomes. While the rich were getting richer, the poor were getting poorer. Luther's description of how interest contracts worked in medieval Germany reinforced the point. He saw the rich lending money and having guaranteed returns while the borrowers took all the risk.[8] It was entirely possible that the borrowers could not repay the loan because of physical injury that prevented them from working or poor economic conditions that hurt their businesses. In either case, the borrowers would not make money but the lenders would still expect the repayment or interest. Compassion and understanding were not part of the contract.

Luther believed that Christians should not engage in ventures that make people worse off. The lending practices of his day certainly made it highly likely that people would be worse off as a result of their borrowing. It was common for people, including church officials, to take advantage of the poor through manipulative lending practices. The easy credit policies of modern America raise similar concerns. How easy it is to abuse credit and become insolvent. The questions of who gets credit and under what conditions remain easily ignored business decisions when profit maximization is the primary focus.

It is interesting to note that Luther saw a direct connection between manipulative, unjust, and unfair business practices and the increasing willingness to sue the courts to settle disputes. What made lawsuits even more despicable was that they were nothing more than tools used by the rich to extract the last cent from a precious soul bought and paid for by the blood of Christ.[9] Questionable as it is, the use of lawsuits as a business strategy remains with us to this day.

Few of us will deny the corrosive effects that sin has on market activity. Given that reality, it is rather amazing how much confidence we have in the ability of markets to solve vexing social problems. The school voucher/choice program in Milwaukee is a good example of a market-based solution. By introducing competition for students, school administrators will be motivated to improve educational quality. Perhaps this is true, but it seems to ignore the inherent sinfulness of all the players in the market. Does competition improve educational quality or does it simply provide a means for crafty actors to advance personal agendas? If history is any guide, both are probably true. So, relying on market-based solutions alone is probably not a good idea.

It is the inherent sinfulness of economic actors that led Luther to conclude that the government should play an active role in the economy. Luther's distrust of competitive market pricing for consumer goods and services led him to argue that the government should "appoint wise and honest men to compute the costs of all sorts of wares and accordingly set prices which would enable the merchant to get along and provide him with an adequate living."[10] As economic policy, this is dubious advice. However, it does highlight the inability of the market to guarantee justice and fairness for all participants. According to Luther, other legitimate roles for the government in the economy include eliminating monopolies,[11] regulating fair trade practices,[12] and providing for the poor.[13]

If anything, Luther's description of life in the 1520s is a reminder that market forces will not improve the moral health of a society. Markets and trade can lead to higher standards of living in material terms. But our sinful behavior will always tempt us to lie, cheat, steal, and take advantage of those who are the least able to protect themselves. When we compete in the marketplace, it is too easy to see the sacrifice of Christ as having no economic value and, therefore, not worth possessing. Luther boldly and unequivocally challenges us today not to make such a mistake.

TEN
LOOKING for the right answers

"Judge for yourselves whether it is right in God's sight to obey you rather than God." —Apostles Peter and John speaking to the teachers of the law (Acts 4:19)

In this chapter, we will discuss some of the current issues that raise questions about ethical business practices. After I describe each issue, I offer several discussion questions. These questions are intended to give us a place to start analyzing the cases. Following these questions, I provide my views. But keep in mind that my goal is to raise all the pertinent issues rather than to necessarily answer all the questions.

> **Topic 1:** *Genesis 1:26,27: Then God said, "Let us make man in our image, in our likeness, and let them rule over the fish of the sea and the birds of the air, over the livestock, over all the earth, and over all the creatures that move along the ground."*

In 1975 Exxon Coal and Minerals Company announced that it had discovered an ore deposit located five miles south of Crandon, in Forest County, Wisconsin. The ore body held copper, gold, lead, silver, and zinc. Some described this particular ore body as one of the largest ever discovered in North America. Exxon began applying for permits that would have allowed it to develop a mine. Given an expected life of 28 years, the mine would have yielded 55 million tons of zinc, lead, and copper—in total worth $4 billion.

A major selling point for the proposed mine was the positive economic impact it would have on the immediate area. A spokesman for the mine estimated that the company would purchase approximately $43 million in materials and supplies during the three-year construction period. Total purchases within the state of Wisconsin were expected to be around $39 million. An additional $147 million would be spent on supplies and materials outside of the state. Once the mine was operating, the company expected to purchase $1.2 million worth of materials per year during the 28-year life of the mine. State tax revenues from the mine were projected to exceed $100 million.

Opening the mine would create four hundred new, permanent jobs. Of those, only 191 would be in mine or mill operations. The rest would be administrative, supervisory, clerical, and maintenance positions. Average wages at the plant would be $15 per hour. In addition, the local economy would add three hundred new jobs to support the mine employees. These jobs would include such service industries as health care, education, retail, food service, and construction.[1]

But the mine proposal created quite a controversy. The mine site is an area rich with scenic beauty and natural resources. Anglers and canoeists are attracted to the pristine lakes and streams. The 223-mile Wolf River is one of the finest trout streams in Wisconsin. In addition, hunters, hikers, and other outdoor enthusiasts enjoy exploring the vast forests located in the county. The Nicolet National Forest alone covers over half of the county's 665,600 acres.

Despite its abundance of natural resources, Forest County remains one of the poorest counties in Wisconsin. At the height of the controversy, Forest County's per capita adjusted gross income ranked 70th out of 72 counties.[2] Wage rates also consistently lagged behind the rest of the state, reaching to only 65.3 percent of the state average.[3] In addition to this, the unemployment rate was substantially higher than the Wisconsin average. About 17.3 percent of the population of Forest County was living below the poverty line, compared to a state average of 10.9 percent.[4]

The proposed underground mine would have covered 550 acres. Safely disposing of the mine wastes was a major concern. The original plan called for 220 acres of the 550-acre site to be used as a "tailings management area."[5] It was estimated that the mine would eventually produce close to 45 million tons of waste rock.[6] Nicolet Minerals Company proposed burying most of the rock in the mine. However, approximately 22 million tons of tailings would have had to be stored in a 90-foot-deep surface pit.[7] The pit would have been lined with plastic and would have been sealed to prevent the tailings from coming into contact with oxygen and water. Due to the high sulfur content of the tailings, exposure to air and water would produce sulfuric acid, an obvious environmental hazard.

Under pressure from critics, Nicolet Minerals Company announced late in 1998 that it had devised a new plan for disposing of the tailings. The company proposed reprocessing the waste rock, thereby eliminating 9 percent of the pyrite.[8] Pyrite is a naturally occurring yellow mineral high in sulfur. The reprocessed waste would be mixed with cement and stored in the mine. Calling the plan experimental, environmental groups such as the Sierra Club were less than impressed.[9]

Issues concerning potential water pollution also drew criticism. Because the mine would be underground, water would tend to leak into it. The water would come from surface sources, such as lakes, streams, and rivers, as well as underground aquifers. Mine officials expected they would have to pump about one million gallons a day from the mine.[10] Because the water would likely be exposed to sulfur, silt, and other chemicals from the mining process, company officials originally proposed piping the water 38 miles, so it could be discharged into the Wisconsin River.[11] Later a new method for handling the wastewater was proposed. Instead of piping the water to the Wisconsin River, the firm planned to build a wastewater treatment facility on-site. This treatment plant would clean the water to standards that would exceed those currently in place for drinking water. The water would then be sent through underground pipes for reabsorption into the environment. In addition, cement would be forced into any cracks that might be found in the mine walls. By filling the cracks with grout, water would not be able to leak into the mine.[12] Environmental groups argued that this was "nothing more than the experiment of the month," which might not even work.[13] Based on these facts, consider the following questions:

1. Balancing the economic need of the community with the potential to damage the environment, would you recommend that the Crandon mine be built?

2. God wants us to be good stewards of his creation. How do Christians balance the need for natural resources like copper and oil with the need to protect environmentally sensitive areas like the Wolf River?

God made it clear from the very beginning that the earth and all that it contains belong to him. David testified to that fact in Psalm 24:1, "The earth is the LORD's, and everything in it, the world, and all who live in it." We as humans have no right to think that we can exploit the earth for our own personal gain. God has given us the privilege and responsibility of managing the earth for our good and his glory. When we pollute, degrade the environment, and destroy what God entrusted to us, we are mismanaging his resources and defying his intentions. Because we know that the creation is a gift from God, Christian business leaders will view environmental concerns as stewardship issues.

In the written record of his Word, Jesus often speaks about our stewardship of God's creation. He especially wants us to remember that what we have is not the result of our own work. Rather, it comes as a blessing from God with a higher purpose than simply to satisfy our desires—to think otherwise is to praise ourselves at God's expense and to misuse his blessings. Christ explained the folly of such a course in the parable of the rich fool (Luke 12:15-21).

Nowhere does Scripture insinuate that using the earth's resources in a God-pleasing manner will result in a shortage. In fact, in the parable of the ten minas (Luke 19:11-27), Jesus taught that God blesses us as we use his creation to serve him. And the words of the psalmist encourage us with the reminder that we can use God's resources to serve him, because he will take care of our needs: "I was young and now I am old, yet I have never seen the righteous forsaken or their children begging bread" (Psalm 37:25).

At the time of Moses, God made it clear that our focus should be on obeying him. He will take care of our provisions. "Follow my decrees and be careful to obey my laws, and you will live safely in the land. Then the land will yield its fruit, and you will eat your fill and live there in safety (Leviticus 25:18,19). Our material well-being is not dependent on our abilities but on his grace. He commands us to obey him and, as we do, to trust that he will "open the heavens, the storehouse of his bounty" (Deuteronomy 28:12). The earth will fail to provide for us only when we turn our backs on our Creator and bring his judgment upon ourselves.

Our understanding that everything we have comes from God helps us recognize that the care of the environment is a stewardship issue. Whether drilling for oil in the Arctic National Wildlife Refuge, building nuclear power plants in California, or mining for ore in Crandon, the Christian needs to keep in mind that God owns the land and all its resources. A willingness to destroy the environment for personal gain stems from sinful motives.

To what degree people should exploit the earth's resources, however, is an open question. The technology that was proposed for the Crandon mine would have made it one of the most advanced, state-of-the-art mines in the world. However, that would have offered little consolation if something had gone wrong and an important watershed had been damaged.

The pages of recent history relate numerous stories that highlight the cost of careless and selfish uses of our resources. When the Exxon Valdez ran aground, millions of gallons of crude oil were dumped into a pristine Alaskan environment. Union Carbide's chemical plant in Bhopal, India, released a cloud of chlorine gas that killed thousands of people. A nuclear power plant at Three Mile Island in Pennsylvania came close to melting down in the late 1970s. The effects could have been deadly. Each of these facilities most likely employed modern technology that was meant to protect the environment. Yet, the accidents occurred, either because of sloppy management or disregard for safety. Cutting corners to save money on safety measures was the likely cause of the accident in Bhopal. Captain Hazelwood's drunkenness likely contributed to the crash of the Exxon Valdez. In a sinful world, accidents are going to happen, but these accidents betrayed careless attitudes in regard to God's creation. These accidents also renewed the debate about corporate America's responsibility to the environment.

Christians need to use common sense and examine their motives before engaging in any project. If the initiative is likely to damage the environment, tough choices will have to be made. When the decision to go ahead with a project is motivated by the desire to make a fast buck, the project is suspect. However, if, after meeting all legal requirements and taking all reasonable precautions, the Christian believes that a project is safe and will benefit people, the Christian is free to undertake the project. The important thing is that he or she recognizes that the environment is God's property. None of us would borrow a friend's car, smash it, and then return it without offering to make restitution. Each of us should take the same approach to business and the environment.

> **Topic 2:** 1 Peter 2:9-12: *You are a chosen people, a royal priesthood, a holy nation, a people belonging to God, that you may declare the praises of him who called you out of darkness into his wonderful light. Once you were not a people, but now you are the people of God; once you had not received mercy, but now you have received mercy. Dear friends, I urge*

you, as aliens and strangers in the world, to abstain from sinful desires, which war against your soul. Live such good lives among the pagans that, though they accuse you of doing wrong, they may see your good deeds and glorify God on the day he visits us.

Proverbs 14:5: A truthful witness does not deceive, but a false witness pours out lies.

16:11: Honest scales and balances are from the LORD; all the weights in the bag are of his making.

19:5: A false witness will not go unpunished, and he who pours out lies will not go free.

21:6: A fortune made by a lying tongue is a fleeting vapor and a deadly snare.

You are probably familiar with the Publishers Clearing House (PCH) sweepstakes and the tantalizing prospect that the Prize Patrol might stop at your house to drop off a $10 million check. The company began its now famous sweepstakes in 1967 as a way to "draw attention to the discounted magazine deals" it offered. According to the company, it has awarded over $135 million in prizes. Forty percent of the company's profits are given to charity.[14] Why, then, was PCH the subject of a lawsuit brought by 24 states and the District of Columbia?

Key to the state of Wisconsin's lawsuit against PCH was the charge that the company "creates and manipulates the content of its solicitations . . . to exploit particular concerns of the elderly for financial independence, religious observance (and) desire to be needed and remembered."[15] The Wisconsin attorney general's office alleged that 75 percent of the people spending more than $2,500 on PCH merchandise were over the age of 62. According to the government, this implies that PCH targeted the elderly.[16]

Many elderly people said that by purchasing more magazines, they believed that they would have better chances of winning. Personalized, direct-mail solicitations seemed to encourage the purchases. Solicitations included encouraging statements, such as, "Dave, please keep January 25 at 9:00 P.M. open on your calendar. That's the time we hope to be giving Leonard Srocynski our $10,000,000 Super Prize. . . . I'd like to see the Ten Million Dollars go to one of our valued friends. And no one is more deserving than Leonard Srocynski." The solicitation was made to look as if it were a memo from the contest manager to the director of the Prize Patrol. Prior to receiving this letter, Leonard, age 79, had regularly purchased products from PCH in an effort to improve his chances of winning. He received letters from the company telling him that he had an "exceptional" rating and "elite" status. To Leonard, that implied that if he kept buying more products, he would have an even better chance at winning the $10 million prize. All totaled, Leonard spent approximately $10,000 on his purchases from PCH.[17]

PCH countered that its promotional technique was "all part of the fundamental advertising culture in our country."[18] The goal is to be unique enough so people will remember your product, while at the same time creating a sense of urgency to get people to act. Despite the government's contention, 70 percent of the millions of entries PCH sends out are never returned. Of those entries that are returned, 80 percent represent orders of less than $100 in merchandise annually. About 95 percent order $500 or less.[19] As for the age-discrimination charge, PCH has limited research suggesting that 70 percent of its customers are younger than 65 years old. Since the company didn't solicit the ages of its potential customers, it couldn't have been guilty of targeting the elderly.

In addition, the company has taken steps to ensure that people are not deceived by its advertising campaign. The company attempts to identify those who make frequent purchases in order to remind them that no purchase is necessary to enter the sweepstakes. In fact, the company sends out approximately 125,000 letters annually to remind frequent customers of the policy. If the customer does not appear to understand the promotion, the name is removed from the mailing list.

Approximately six thousand names have already been deleted. PCH also supports legislation that requires prominent *No Purchase Necessary* messages, clear instructions detailing how to enter a sweepstakes with or without an order, and an unambiguous statement outlining the numerical odds of winning.[20]

Questions to consider:

1. What ethical standards should Christian businesspeople follow when marketing their products?

2. What ethical standards can realistically be expected from non-Christian employees?

The Federal Trade Commission (FTC) was created in 1914 to ensure vigorous, free, and fair competition in the marketplace. Section 5 of the FTC Act prohibits unfair and deceptive trade practices. Two specific trade practices that are illegal under Section 5 are false advertising and bait-and-switch schemes. In addition to other remedies, the FTC has the authority to order companies to cease such practices and provide compensation to injured consumers.

To be classified as false advertising, a message must contain (1) information, misinformation, or the omission of information that is likely to mislead a "reasonable consumer" or (2) unsubstantiated claims. A reasonable consumer is characterized by the way an ordinary person would act in similar circumstances. Vague generalities and apparent exaggerations known as puffery are not illegal. If the claim appears to be factual but is not, it may be considered deceptive. For example, a claim that an orange drink is made from 100 percent pure orange concentrate while it actually only contains 10 percent pure concentrate would be illegal. Making an additional claim that the drink will cure cancer when there is no scientific evidence to support that claim might also be considered deceptive advertising.

A bait-and-switch scheme refers to the practice of advertising a product at a very low price and then trying to get the consumer to purchase a more expensive item. (Often the seller doesn't even have the cheaper item in stock.) For the practice to be illegal, the seller must (1) refuse to show the advertised product, (2) fail to have a reasonable amount of inventory on hand at the time the item is advertised, (3) discourage employees from selling the item, or (4) fail to even deliver the advertised item in the future.

Deception undermines relationships between people. Deception also undermines our very relationship with God. Paul pointed out that lying violates the character of the Christian: "Do not lie to each other, since you have taken off your old self with its practices and have put on the new self, which is being renewed in knowledge in the image of its Creator" (Colossians 3:9,10). Christians are to hold themselves to a higher standard. We are to resist the ways of the world and follow the model of Christ. Our focus is to honor and obey the Lord, not to seek selfish gain.

The words of our Lord, as recorded by Paul, provide the context by which Christian business leaders should evaluate their marketing efforts. The Christian sees that marketing is not simply an effort to sell more goods and services. Even the grand-sounding goal of establishing a "relationship" between firm and client falls short of our God-given goal.

Marketing is about truth. The goal of marketing is to convince as many people as possible that they need a product or service. In general, two views of marketing exist. One viewpoint sees marketing or its first cousin, advertising, as nothing more than a way for the firm to manipulate and take advantage of the consumer. A radically different viewpoint regards marketing as the most efficient way to provide the consumer with the vital information he or she needs to make an informed decision. The particular viewpoint we adopt is key to the way we evaluate the ethics that apply to marketing.

The difference is one of deception versus information. If the marketing effort is aimed at deceiving people and tricking them into making a purchase, the Christian would be critical of that effort. However, a marketing campaign aimed at informing the consumer is an entirely different effort. Educating consumers is both economically efficient and in agreement with scriptural principles.

The line between education and deception is not always as clear as we may think it is, however. For example, American Home Products claimed that hospitals were more likely to recommend acetaminophen, "the aspirin-free pain reliever in Anacin-3," than any other pain reliever. The problem is that Tylenol, the drug even more hospitals recommend than Anacin-3, also contains acetaminophen.[21] The general public could not be expected to be aware of this distinction. True or not, the issue is whether the makers of Anacin-3 were massaging the truth for their own personal gain.

In the United States, the Federal Trade Commission is responsible for ensuring that the public is protected against "unfair or deceptive acts or practices."[22] But providing clear definitions of what constitutes "unfair" or "deceptive" practices is not easy. The FTC accepts some exaggeration in advertising as acceptable. Puffery, which describes clearly exaggerated statements, is not illegal. For example, the claim that if your son eats one raw egg a day, he will become as smart as a Nobel laureate is an exaggeration no reasonable person would believe. As such, all else being equal, the claim would probably not violate federal law. It would seem unlikely that anyone would be deceived by that statement.

We may debate whether puffery is an acceptable business practice for Christians. As we have previously seen, if deception is employed, Christians should think twice about being involved. This, then, requires that we define *deception*. Creating an illusion or committing fraud involves manipulating people. *Manipulation* may be defined as "getting people to do what you want without resorting to force or logic." Credit card advertisements often resort to creating an illusion. How many of us haven't received a "pre-approved" platinum card with no annual fee and a 2.9 percent interest rate? Only when we read the fine print do we find out that those benefits are valid for only a limited time. Unless we thoroughly study all the information, we might actually believe that we are going to get a free, low-rate credit card.

What one consumer considers manipulative or deceptive, another may not. Therefore, the Christian marketing representative will want to be doubly careful when promoting a product or service. Our goal, as Christians, is not the same as that of other people. Because Christ died for our sins, eternal salvation is ours. The ultimate goal is not earthly wealth but eternal life. We want to keep our eyes on that goal, even as we conduct our business. In fact, that goal will be the foundation of everything we do. A Christian will not search out the most vulnerable in the marketplace just to earn a fast buck. Christ came to earth to serve, not to be served. Christian business leaders will not abandon his example.

> **Topic 3:** *Galatians 5:13-15: You, my brothers, were called to be free. But do not use your freedom to indulge the sinful nature; rather, serve one another in love. The entire law is summed up in a single command: "Love your neighbor as yourself." If you keep on biting and devouring each other, watch out or you will be destroyed by each other.*

The city of Milwaukee, Wisconsin, has a problem with lead poisoning, which can cause mental and physical disabilities in children. In 1992, 73 percent of children who were tested for lead had elevated levels in their blood. That figure dropped to 16 percent in 2000, compared to the national average of 4.4 percent.[23] But 16 percent still equates to approximately 5,750 kids.

At issue is who should clean up the problem. Since approximately 40,000 homes might be affected, the total cost of a cleanup could exceed $100 million.[24] In October 2000, the Milwaukee City Council voted to sue the paint industry for the cost of the cleanup. Industry officials maintain that they are not to blame. Federal law did not ban lead in paint until 1950.

Because lead was no longer used in the manufacturing of paint after that time, the industry argues that it should not be held responsible. Critics of the paint industry counter that the industry knew of the dangers long before it finally removed the lead. They maintain that the industry's failure to act makes the industry responsible.

Questions to consider:

1. Can Christians effectively participate in a competitive marketplace if they are supposed to look out for the interests of others?

2. How much responsibility should a Christian business leader assume for a company's past mistakes?

"Then Moses went up to God, and the LORD called to him from the mountain and said, 'This is what you are to say to the house of Jacob and what you are to tell the people of Israel: "You yourselves have seen what I did to Egypt, and how I carried you on eagles' wings and brought you to myself. Now if you obey me fully and keep my covenant, then out of all nations you will be my treasured possession. Although the whole earth is mine, you will be for me a kingdom of priests and a holy nation"'" (Exodus 19:3-6). God spoke these words just before he established his covenant with the Israelites at Mount Sinai. He was reminding them of the great things he had done for them. They would show their appreciation for what he had done by keeping the commandments that he was about to give them. As a community of believers, they learned that they were to show respect for one another and for God and to look out for their neighbors.

Isaiah describes God as "a God of justice" (Isaiah 30:18). Justice can be measured by how a society protects its most vulnerable members. "Do not exploit the poor because they are poor and do not crush the needy in court, for the LORD will take up their case and will plunder those who plunder them" (Proverbs 22:22,23). As Christ lives in us, we will not just worry about our own self-interests. We will protect the vulnerable as well. The prophet Micah sums up our relationship with others and God: "He has showed you, O man, what is good. And what does the LORD require of you? To act justly and to love mercy and to walk humbly with your God" (6:8). For Christians living in a competition-driven market economy, the trick is how to balance our own self-interests with our need to help and protect those around us.

Christ himself taught a lesson about helping the less fortunate in society. One day an "expert in the law" pressed Jesus for a definition of *neighbor*. The man wanted to be sure he was keeping God's precept about loving your neighbor as yourself. Jesus responded by telling the famous parable of the good Samaritan (Luke 10:25-37). It became clear even to the expert in the law that the neighbor was "the one who had mercy on him." Christ concluded by telling the expert, "Go and do likewise."

The parable of the good Samaritan is deceptively easy to understand. As Christ tells the parable, we can almost feel the expert in the law becoming uncomfortable as he hears what Christ is saying. Few people would miss the point that God expects us to help those in need. And we do that gladly because we know that God helped us in our greatest need by giving his life so that we might have eternal life. To grasp the depth of the parable, remember that Jews held the Samaritans in open contempt. When Christ praised the actions of a despicable outsider, the slam dunk was complete. Just as Christ died for all people, we are to help all those in need, regardless of their stations or nationalities. The "expert" didn't look so smart after Christ was finished.

Perhaps we need to put ourselves in the expert's sandals and ask ourselves, Who are our neighbors? My dad used to say, "Talk is cheap. It takes money to buy whiskey." Most Christian grade school children could tell you the meaning of the parable of the good Samaritan. The trick for Christian business leaders is to apply that parable to life in a marketplace driven by competition. When it comes to lead paint, how much responsibility does a Christian business leader assume? Of course, lead paint is just one topic of controversy. As Christians, how far do we go to help and protect the consuming public?

As we look for answers to that question, we keep in mind that God allows us to make money—to pursue profitable business ventures.

This point is important because it is easy to fall into the trap of believing that earning a profit is somehow unclean. It doesn't have to be. The good Samaritan obviously had earned money to spare—he used it to care for the beaten stranger. God expects us to work to support ourselves and our families. Blessing us so that we profit from business is one of the ways he provides for us. Paul explained the value of work in 1 Thessalonians 4:11,12: "Make it your ambition to lead a quiet life, to mind your own business and to work with your hands, just as we told you, so that your daily life may win the respect of outsiders and so that you will not be dependent on anybody." If God chooses to bless our efforts with material blessings, we should not be ashamed or embarrassed. Obviously, we will not want to gloat or allow the blessings to obstruct our faith. If we accept the blessings for what they are—gifts from God to use in a God-pleasing way—we can rejoice and use them to advance his kingdom.

One way we advance our Lord's kingdom is by helping the less fortunate or the vulnerable. In the case of lead poisoning, Christian businesspeople can advance the work of the Lord in at least two ways. One way is by making sure that their products don't contain lead or anything else that can harm God's creation. The second way is by sharing their blessings to help those in need.

In our discussion of the Crandon mining controversy, we established that God does not prohibit us from using his creation to improve the condition of all people. The fact is that sometimes, despite our best intentions, we will do things that cause more harm than good. In the 1960s, women were given thalidomide to blunt some of the negative effects of a difficult pregnancy. But the drug caused grotesque birth defects. As

Christians, we have a responsibility to make sure that we produce and market only those products that are safe and beneficial to society. This implies also that we will continually improve our products by incorporating the latest technology in our designs and production methods. If it becomes apparent that our product or service is unreasonably dangerous, as Christians, we will do everything possible to correct the problem.

Notice that we are using terms such as *unreasonable, safe, beneficial,* and *latest technology.* The meanings of these words are imprecise and open to debate. But God expects us to use our sanctified common sense to do what is right. If we find out that our paint is dangerous, we have an obligation to make it safe and to help clean up the danger that we caused. Since modern corporations very well might outlive their managers, the obligation does not cease when one generation of decision-makers is gone. If the company was clearly in the wrong when the decision was made, succeeding generations still have the responsibility to help repair the damage.

But what should a Christian do if cleaning up a past problem would lead to bankruptcy? Several years ago, Ford Motor Company spent close to $3 billion recalling Firestone tires that may have been defective.[25] Even for a company like Ford, $3 billion was a lot of money. Does a good Samaritan have to be willing to bankrupt the company? After all, if the company goes bankrupt, the injured may never be helped.

A related question is, How do we know when to admit that a product or service is defective or harmful to God's creation? Earlier we asked how many people would have to die before a Christian would order a recall. At that time we skirted the issue. Now we need to answer it. I would have hated to be the president of Ford or Firestone when the accident reports started to filter into his office, suggesting that his products might be killing his customers. Ford finally ordered a recall after approximately 80 people had died. Was that too late? It took time to gather scientific evidence to establish a cause for action. Meanwhile, more people may have died.

The question isn't easy to answer. We do kno
creation depends on God for its continued exist
LORD, you preserve both man and beast" (Psalm 3t
does not mean that people are puppets of God. As ⌐ve so
clearly showed in the Garden of Eden, we have a free will that
can and does get us into all kinds of trouble. Yet nothing in
the universe happens outside of God's control. Christ
reaffirmed this when he asked, "Are not two sparrows sold for
a penny? Yet not one of them will fall to the ground apart
from the will of your Father. And even the very hairs of your
head are all numbered" (Matthew 10:29,30). When troubling
things happen, the apostle Paul reassures us, "We know that in
all things God works for the good of those who love him,
who have been called according to his purpose" (Romans
8:28). We will not be able to pinpoint the exact time when a
decision like a tire recall should be made. But we can pray that
God will keep sinful thoughts and motives from our hearts as
we make our decisions and that he will guide us to make the
decisions that are best for his kingdom. And we can make
such decisions secure in the knowledge that God is guiding
our judgment.

Christians need to ponder still another question: What
responsibility do we have to those who are hurting when our
business had nothing to do with the cause of their pain and
suffering? Frame that question in the context of the lead-
paint controversy. How much responsibility should a
Christian businessperson assume if his or her paint business
started well after lead paint was outlawed? Christ's point in
the parable of the good Samaritan is that everyone in need is
our neighbor. Because of the grace God has bestowed upon
us, we will want to honor him through our good works. "Let
your light shine before men, that they may see your good
deeds and praise your Father in heaven" (Matthew 5:16). This
could mean using some of our company's resources to help
those in need, even if we did not cause the problem. Our
helpful attitude is driven by love for our Lord, not self-
aggrandizement or the desire to increase our profit potential.

A difficult issue for me is to know how much to give. Business can be cutthroat and very uncertain. The business horizon is littered with thousands of companies that failed. Venerable companies like TWA, Penn Central, and Pan Am were at one time household names. Now they no longer exist. Whether a business is large or small, competition in the economic marketplace can be vicious. As Christians, we want to help the less fortunate. How do we know if we will have enough to give to charity when economic conditions can change almost overnight? In the Old Testament, God set one tenth of the income as the required gift. Clearly, he does not require us to give so much to the poor that we become one of the needy. But he does want us to trust him. Because of our sinful nature, decisions that require trust are often the most difficult business decisions we have to make. Yet if we fail to place our trust in God, then we are making a god of our own intellect and our own skills. Those false gods offer no peace or comfort.

> ***Topic 4:*** *Philippians 2:1-8: If you have any encouragement from being united with Christ, if any comfort from his love, if any fellowship with the Spirit, if any tenderness and compassion, then make my joy complete by being like-minded, having the same love, being one in spirit and purpose. Do nothing out of selfish ambition or vain conceit, but in humility consider others better than yourselves. Each of you should look not only to your own interests, but also to the interests of others. Your attitude should be the same as that of Christ Jesus: Who, being in very nature God, did not consider equality with God something to be grasped, but made himself nothing, taking the very nature of a servant, being made in human likeness. And being found in appearance as a man, he humbled himself and became obedient to death—even death on a cross!*

Kohl's Department Store has become one of the fastest growing retailers in America. In 2000, the company employed

43,000 employees and operated 320 stores. Those stores earned $258 million on $4.6 billion in sales.[26] By 2004, the company operated almost seven hundred stores.

Like other retailers, Kohl's purchases some of its apparel from a Taiwanese firm that operates a factory in Nicaragua. Specifically, the firm sells jeans to Kohl's for approximately $7. Kohl's then sells those same jeans to consumers for around $17.[27]

Torn by civil war and plagued with natural disasters, Nicaragua is a very poor country. Its gross domestic product (GDP) of $2.24 billion pales compared to the almost $9 trillion American economy. To put that in human terms, GDP per capita in Nicaragua is $460 per person. In the United States, the figure is closer to $34,000. The minimum wage in Nicaragua is $61 a month, with the average monthly wage reaching about $100 per month.[28] Comparatively speaking, employees making jeans for Kohl's are better off than their counterparts. Employees are paid based upon the number of jeans that they handle. The average wage at the factory is approximately $150 per month. With bonuses and overtime, some employees earn as much as $271 every two weeks.[29]

Some Americans view this as exploitation. The National Labor Committee (NLC), a labor rights organization, has chosen to boycott Kohl's in an attempt to improve the plight of Nicaraguan laborers. The NLC estimates that labor costs approximately 20 cents per pair of jeans produced in Nicaragua. They would like Kohl's to use its influence to get that figure increased to 28 cents.[30] They also want Kohl's to do more to improve working conditions in Nicaragua. The NLC alleges that employees are fired illegally, abused emotionally and physically, denied bathroom breaks, and forced to work mandatory overtime. Specifically, the NLC wants fired labor leaders rehired.

Kohl's has investigated the claims and has determined that working conditions at the plant are acceptable. The company steadfastly refuses to get involved in any labor disputes, maintaining that this is a third-party issue. Economists also question the wisdom of increasing wages at the factory. Some economists argue that raising wages will just force the owners of the company to move the factory to China, where the wages are substantially lower still.[31]

Questions to consider:

1. What responsibility do businesses owe a community?

2. As a Christian, do you believe that Kohl's is exploiting Nicaraguan labor?

The ability to balance the self-interest of economic theory with the servant's attitude of Christianity demands Solomon-like wisdom. During the last half of the 20th century and the first part of the 21st century, the American political machine has been searching for the point of equilibrium between these two views. Changes in the minimum wage, mandated benefits like family leave and medical leave, and welfare reform are all attempts to encourage individual initiative while providing a helping hand for those in need. Without Solomon to guide us, the debate will never end.

The Kohl's example is an international application of a very real domestic problem. The distribution of income between the richest and poorest Americans is the most unequal in history. The richest 20 percent of Americans are now estimated to control 50 percent of the nation's wealth. Similarly, at least according to Congressman Martin Sabo of Minnesota, "between 1977 and 1994, the average after tax income of the top 1 percent of American families rose by 72%, while that of the poorest fifth dropped by 16%."[32] Whether or not Congressman Sabo's analysis is correct, today 44 percent of Americans do believe that the disparity between the haves and have nots in this country is growing. In 1988, 26 percent of Americans believed that.[33] Poorer Americans are working hard to provide society with material benefits that they themselves can't necessarily enjoy. Likewise, while employees in Nicaragua are helping make Kohl's economically successful, the employees themselves aren't necessarily prospering.

Nehemiah was disturbed by what he found when he returned to Jerusalem (chapter 5). Not only was the city in ruins, but many of its citizens were desperately poor. To make matters worse, countrymen were exacting fees and taxes that prevented the poor from ever hoping to become economically self-sufficient. Nehemiah was experiencing an economic system that was out of control. Usury and the practice of selling people into slavery had become acceptable economic transactions. While some benefited, many others did not. Nehemiah was firm and unequivocal when he said, "What you are doing is not right. Shouldn't you walk in the fear of our God to avoid the reproach of our Gentile enemies?" (verse 9). Concerned for the plight of the poor, Nehemiah instituted reforms that prevented the rich and powerful from exploiting the poor and vulnerable.

The fact that an individual or a corporation is rich and powerful doesn't mean that it is exploiting the masses. We have what we have, not because of our own efforts but because of God's grace. Through Joshua, God reminded the Israelites and reminds us that this is true: "I gave you a land on which you did not toil and cities you did not build; and you live in them and eat from vineyards and olive groves that you did not plant" (Joshua 24:13). The very blessings God has bestowed on us through his grace will make us want to give thanks to him. And one of the reasons God has blessed us is so that we might be generous. "You will be made rich in every way so that you can be generous on every occasion, and through us your generosity will result in thanksgiving to God. This service that you perform is not only supplying the needs of God's people but is also overflowing in many expressions of thanks to God. Because of the service by which you have proved yourselves, men will praise God for the obedience that accompanies your confession of the gospel of Christ, and for your generosity in sharing with them and with everyone else" (2 Corinthians 9:11-13). By sharing our undeserved blessings, we will help expand the kingdom of God.

Even when we know what is true and right, it can be difficult to know how to apply that knowledge. Kohl's could accept a lower profit margin and raise the wage rate for Nicaraguan employees. But there is no guarantee that it would improve the plight of the local employees if Kohl's insisted that the factory pay higher wages. The factory might simply move to another location in a different country. Under that scenario, Kohl's generosity would make conditions worse for the very people it is trying to help. Some might argue that Kohl's should just stop doing business with such firms. The counterargument is that if Kohl's doesn't do business with these suppliers, the plight of the local residents will never improve. Kohl's trade does result in a higher relative standard of living for local residents. It is reasonable to conclude that if Kohl's were not buying these jeans, these people would be relatively worse off. Because we live in a sinful world, the most efficient and effective way to share our blessings is not always clear.

We are able to exercise the free will God has given us according to the economic doctrine of self-interest. Because of his grace, we may prosper materially. Simply giving our possessions to the poor without forethought may not be good stewardship. As in the case of Kohl's, it may be counterproductive. In our sinful world, we may not always feel that we can choose between a good choice and a bad choice. At times we may need to choose between a bad choice and a less-bad choice. Choosing the lesser of two evils may be our only option. At least, as Christians, we have the comfort of knowing that God will make all things work to his glory.

> **Topic 5:** *Proverbs 31:8,9: Speak up for those who cannot speak for themselves, for the rights of all who are destitute. Speak up and judge fairly; defend the rights of the poor and needy.*
>
> *Job 29:12-17: Because I rescued the poor who cried for help, and the fatherless who had none to assist him. The man who was dying blessed me; I made the widow's heart sing. I put on righteousness as my clothing; justice*

was my robe and my turban. I was eyes to the blind and feet to the lame. I was a father to the needy; I took up the case of the stranger. I broke the fangs of the wicked and snatched the victims from their teeth.

President Clinton promised to "end welfare as we know it." Wisconsin Governor Tommy Thompson helped do that when his version of welfare reform, Wisconsin Works, was approved by the Wisconsin legislature in 1997. Wisconsin Works, or W-2, fundamentally shifted the focus of public assistance programs in Wisconsin. Under the old Aid to Families with Dependent Children program, any adult with a dependent child could apply for state assistance through county social service agencies. If the applicant met certain income, asset, and residency requirements, the person would be eligible for a cash payment. For a family of three, this meant $517 in cash and $103 in food stamps.[34]

Under W-2, the focus is on "improving the capacity of adults for self-support."[35] By giving the disadvantaged the skills they need to compete in the marketplace, they become self-sufficient and no longer need public assistance. To accomplish this goal, cash assistance is linked to a full-time work requirement. Most people who don't find employment will not receive public support. Those who do can apply for subsidized child care, health, and training benefits. Basically, W-2 is a market approach that denies that welfare is an entitlement. "The W-2 reward system is designed to reinforce behavior that leads to independence and self-sufficiency."[36]

W-2 was able to be implemented because various public, non-profit, and for-profit agencies were allowed to bid on the right to manage the program. Those agencies that were awarded state contracts became responsible for administering the program. In return for moving people from welfare to work, the agencies could earn a profit on the contract. If the incurred costs were less than the amount bid, the state allowed the agency to keep at least some of the difference. By the end of the first year, the *Wisconsin State Journal* reported, "Private agencies that administer the state's welfare reform program in nine counties plan to pocket $9.4 million in profits from money left over from the initiative's first year."[37] Some people were uncomfortable with the idea that private agencies were profiting from public welfare programs. Nonetheless, by September of 1998, only 10,047 families were receiving cash assistance, compared with 34,491 families in September of 1997.[38]

The question of involving private agencies in welfare reform posed one other problem for W-2 supporters. The legislature's Joint Audit Committee found that the for-profit agency provider Maximus had made over $400,000 in questionable W-2 related expenditures.[39] A second provider, the non-profit Employment Solutions, was accused of improperly billing the state more than $140,000.

Questions to consider:

1. Can social service programs be efficiently and fairly administered by private firms on a for-profit basis?

2. What should be the role of business in providing social service programs?

Jesus noted that poverty will never go away (Matthew 26:11). The real question facing society is, How do we manage the problem? Is poverty an individual issue or a social problem? An individual approach to poverty would require that each member of society get involved and help those in need. Socializing the problem forces government to provide solutions. As Christians living and working in a market economy, we must find the proper balance between individual and government action.

One challenge in trying to address the problem of poverty is that those in need do not walk around with signs readily identifying their plight. Many people are truly in need but are too proud to ask for help. Some simply do not have the physical or mental capabilities to support themselves. Changing economic circumstances have hurt others. A good friend of mine was nearly bankrupted by the 1980–1981 recession. To make matters worse, at the same time, he was hospitalized for kidney stones. Without health insurance but with the responsibility of three daughters to feed, he was on the verge of bankruptcy and needed to apply for food stamps. Through no fault of his own, my friend became financially poor. Many people are in the same situation. Because we want to be good stewards of our resources and because we want the government to be good stewards of our resources, we want to make sure that the help goes to those who truly need it.

It is tempting to turn a cold shoulder to the plight of the needy, because those that abuse the welfare system are such visible targets. I had my freshman economics class balance the federal budget for a class project one year. The two most popular programs to cut were foreign aid and welfare spending. For this class project, welfare was defined as Aid to Families with Dependent Children (AFDC). That program typically provided direct cash payments to mothers so they could raise their children. There is no doubt that the program was abused through the years. One problem with the proposal to help balance the budget by cutting welfare spending is that AFDC represents less than one percent of the federal budget. If we want to save money, other programs would allow for more substantial cuts. A second problem is that not everyone on AFDC is a slacker. One young lady in that economics class had firsthand experience with the program. She recounted how it had helped her family achieve self-sufficiency. Stereotyping people does not help. The point is that we simply cannot afford to throw the baby out with the bathwater.

Scripture demands that we help those in need. It also demands that those who are capable should work. "If a man will not work, he shall not eat" (2 Thessalonians 3:10). We could argue that the anti-poverty Great Society programs failed because they lacked a work requirement. From that standpoint, Wisconsin's W-2 program is a step in the right direction. I will be the first to concede that W-2 is not the perfect answer to poverty. But Christians need to understand the importance of work. We should not rely on others if we are capable of supporting ourselves.

There will be those times, though, when Christians will need outside help. The instructions God gave in Leviticus 19—to leave some of the harvest for the poor—demonstrate the compassion we are to have for the needy. Paul's words to the Corinthians (1 Corinthians 16:1-4) remind us that the church also has a role to play in helping the needy.

Knowing that we have a responsibility to help the poor is a far cry from knowing what that obligation entails. Christian business leaders need to understand that God expects us, individually and collectively, to help those in need, especially our brothers and sisters in the faith who are in need. The instructions in Leviticus remind us that profit maximization is not our only goal on this earth. Some of our corporate resources could best be spent helping our fellow Christians. I think Paul's instructions to the congregation in Corinth also need to be reexamined. American business has been richly blessed. God expects us to use that wealth for more than personal pleasure. We, as Christians, know that our businesses are tools that can be used for the benefit of God's kingdom.

Topic 6: *Proverbs 12:22: The* LORD *detests lying lips, but he delights in men who are truthful.*

Acts 5:3,4: Then Peter said, "Ananias, how is it that Satan has so filled your heart that you have lied to the Holy Spirit and have kept for yourself some of the money you received for the land? Didn't it belong to you before it was sold? And after it was sold, wasn't the money at your disposal? What made you think of doing such a thing? You have not lied to men but to God."

What became known as the Seinfeld case began in Milwaukee in 1993. Jerry Mackenzie, an executive at Miller Brewing Company, referenced a sexually explicit episode of the popular television show while talking to a coworker. The coworker was offended and filed a complaint. Mackenzie was fired because "the 'Seinfeld' incident was the culmination of a pattern of inappropriate behavior, which included an earlier complaint of sexual harassment, made by his secretary."[40] He sued for wrongful discharge and was awarded $24.7 million. The case was complicated by more than just issues of sexual harassment. It seems that in 1987, Miller Brewing had reorganized Mackenzie's job. According to Mackenzie, his "responsibilities were cut and half of the employees he supervised were assigned to another man."[41] At that time his pay grade was not altered, and he was told his promotional opportunities would not be affected. In 1989, Miller Brewing did change the pay level of Mackenzie's job. The change was implemented in 1992, but it seems that no one bothered to tell Mackenzie.[42] The jury decided that this was wrong and ruled in favor of Mackenzie. The Wisconsin Supreme Court didn't agree.

By a 6-0 vote, the Wisconsin Supreme Court decided that employers who lied to their employees were not doing anything illegal. Writing for the majority, Justice Wilcox stated that the court was "apprehensive of interjecting the judiciary between employees and their employers, thereby altering the basic tenets of our labor market and our economy."[43] The court reasoned that if employers were required to tell the whole truth, then employees would be also. By allowing people to sue under such circumstances, the court system would be overwhelmed with a large number of lawsuits.

Questions to consider:

1. Is lying to employees ever permissible?

2. Should the government establish minimum standards for labor contracts?

Employment at will is the common law doctrine that allows employers or employees to terminate an employment relationship for any reason, or no reason, without violating the law. It has been estimated that 60 percent of all private sector employees in the United States are "at-will" employees.[44] Unless employees are covered by a collective bargaining agreement or protected by a specific legal statute or public policy, they have no right to due process regarding their dismissal, even if the employer lies or has no real reason for the dismissal.

One of the saddest days in my retail career occurred at the store I managed in northern California. We had a hard time finding help of any kind. Finding someone who could work as a customer service supervisor was even more difficult. The ideal candidate had to be friendly, organized, capable of dealing with the general public, able to supervise seven cashiers, and willing to work a flexible schedule. We finally found such a person working within another division of our store. When asked if she would be interested in the position, she said she would give it a try. Her only condition was that if she did not like the job after a trial period, she would be able to return to her previous job. We agreed, and she started training just before the Memorial Day weekend.

That particular store sold alcohol, which required that the cashiers ask all customers for identification to ensure they were of the legal drinking age. Our new customer service supervisor, still in training, sold some beer to a customer without checking any identification. The customer happened to be an undercover police officer. Company policy in such a circumstance was to terminate the employee immediately. I felt so bad for this lady. What should have been a win-win situation for her and the store turned into a nightmare. In accordance with the policy, she was terminated instead of being allowed to return to her original position. It just didn't seem right.

Employment at will does not legally obligate the parties of a labor relationship to have just cause when making an employment decision. Just cause essentially means, "having a good reason to take action." Employment at will does not provide the safeguard of fairness (substantive due process). Nor does it provide an established appeal process (procedural due process).

Recent court decisions have limited the scope of application for employment at will. Under the doctrine of implied contract, a handbook may be viewed as a binding contract. Failure to follow printed policies may open the employer to legal liability, even if the employee is "at will." Likewise, the violation of a law, statute, ordinance, or even a public policy may create legal liability for the offending party. An example of a legal statute is the Civil Rights Act of 1964, which prohibits employers from making employment decisions on the basis of gender, religion, race, color, or national origin. An example of public policy protection is the policy that allows employees to participate in jury duty. Failure to protect employees from dismissal while attending jury duty would lessen the desire of people to participate in a fundamental obligation of our legal system.

The doctrine of employment at will can easily be abused. Christian businesspeople realize they must avoid the temptation to exploit their employees. "Masters, provide your slaves with what is right and fair, because you know that you also have a Master in heaven" (Colossians 4:1). We have discussed before how God expects us to treat one another with love and respect. In this passage, that theme is applied specifically to the business relationship.

However, if an employer terminates an employment relationship for no reason or, worse yet, for less-than-justifiable reasons, that employer runs the risk of violating the Eighth Commandment. God told his people, "You shall not give false testimony against your neighbor." Martin Luther defined this commandment as meaning, "We should fear and love God that we do not tell lies about our neighbor, betray him, or give him a bad name, but defend him, speak well of him, and take his words and actions in the kindest possible way."[45]

In the case involving Miller Brewing, the Wisconsin Supreme Court upheld the company's contention that the employee was an "at-will" employee, and thus the employment action was not illegal. It may not have been illegal to cut his pay without telling him, even after promising that his pay would remain the same, but Christian businesspeople are troubled that any kind of lying is accepted. Paul tells us in Ephesians 4:25, "Each of you must put off falsehood and speak truthfully to his neighbor, for we are all members of one body." God does not tolerate lies, deception, or misleading conduct from his people.

Failing to tell an employee the honest truth about his or her job or performance is a cowardly act that flies in the face of Jesus Christ. Christian employers have an obligation, out of love and respect for their God, to treat all employees with dignity, respect, and truthfulness.

In modern society, employment decisions are generally based on the doctrine of just cause. Failure to have a good reason for an employment action may give the world the wrong impression. Many will believe that the employee committed some wrong. If that isn't true, the employer will have contributed to the defamation of the employee's name. Employment decisions require honest motives and pure intent by employers.

> **Topic 7:** *Galatians 3:28: There is neither Jew nor Greek, slave nor free, male nor female, for you are all one in Christ Jesus.*

Beginning August 1, 2000, GM, Ford, and DaimlerChrysler announced that they would begin offering health-care benefits to same-sex partners, over 18 years of age, who had lived together continually for at least six months.[46] Exactly 102 Fortune 500 companies now offer such benefits to their employees. Nationwide, 3,572 employers have granted coverage to domestic partners.[47] As one human resource official at DaimlerChrysler explained, "We just want to attract the brightest talent that values and embraces diversity in the workplace."[48] Ironically, all three companies waited until after their annual meetings to announce the change—in order to avoid giving opponents public forums to criticize their plans.

American opinion regarding homosexuality has undergone a radical transformation in recent years. An Associated Press poll found that 56 percent of Americans support granting gay couples inheritance rights. About 53 percent favor giving them family health benefits. And 50 percent favor giving them social security benefits. Although most American adults still oppose gay marriage (51 percent to 34 percent), 54 percent of adults under the age of 35 do support such marriages.[49] It appears that support for gay rights will increase over time. As one diversity director said, "As the world and workplace changes and becomes more openminded, it's the right decision."[50]

The government is also responding to the changing public views on homosexuality. Milwaukee is now 1 of 50 American cities that allows gay couples to register their partnerships.[51] These registries don't offer any legal benefits, but they do bring the government one step closer to recognizing such unions. The state of Vermont officially extended "the same rights and benefits as opposite sex marriage" when it passed its civil union law.[52]

Questions to consider:

1. Can employment discrimination ever be justified?

2. Should Christian businesspeople resist extending health benefits to gay partners?

The government is an institution created by God to maintain order in a world that has fallen to sin. God grants governments the authority to pass laws (1 Peter 2:13), enforce those laws (John 18:31), and adjudicate matters under the law (1 Peter 2:14). The government also has the right to collect taxes (Matthew 22:15-22), inflict capital punishment (Romans 13:4), and declare war (1 Samuel 15:18). This shows that the government has been created and is ordained with the power to preserve and protect its people. The government has broad powers to do what it wants in promoting the social welfare of society.

We have a responsibility to honor and obey our government. The apostle Paul made it clear that if we disobey our government, we are rebelling against God (Romans 13:1,2). When Paul wrote these words, the Roman government was under the control of nonbelievers. Paul's point is that our obligation to God's institution of government does not depend on the point of view of those currently in power.

When considering the question of benefits for same-sex partners, we need to differentiate between what the government decrees and what we, as Christians, choose to do. Let me explain. If the government mandates that all businesses must offer health-care benefits to the partners of homosexuals, Christians have an obligation to follow the law. If the government does not mandate that all businesses offer health insurance to the partners of homosexuals, Christian business leaders must decide for themselves. Their decision will take several things into account. They know that homosexuality is a sin (1 Corinthians 6:9-11; Leviticus 18:22). They also know that the wages of sin is death—both physical and spiritual death. Consequently, unless the person repents, he or she will have forfeited eternal life and will be lost eternally. From this perspective, homosexuality is no different than any other sin. If the sinner takes delight in sinning and refuses to repent, that person is headed for eternal damnation. The Christian's main concern is that the Holy Spirit has the opportunity to work through the law and gospel to bring the sinner to repentance and to eternal life.

The question the Christian business leader needs to answer is, Is it ethical to offer health-care benefits to same-sex partners? Many argue—with justification—that offering them health-care benefits is wrong because it gives the impression that the business owner condones that lifestyle. It's a matter of giving offense. As Christians, we need to make sure that we do not operate our businesses in a way that would cause "anyone to stumble" (1 Corinthians 10:32). At the same time, we want to make sure that we don't give the impression that this is an unforgivable sin or that this sin is worse than adultery, idolatry, drunkenness, or slander.

Christian business owners will want to approach every decision with thoughtfulness and prayer. And, finally, we must approach every decision with faith in the fact that Christ has saved us from the guilt of our sins and that even our wrong decisions will not disqualify us from eternal life.

This saving faith provides the framework for every one of our tasks on earth. Because we have fallen, the stain of sin will tarnish all our works. But when we live with our eyes of faith focused always on the cross, our heavenly Father sees our lives through the perfection of Christ. Our deeds and decisions are pure in his sight. If we operate our business with humility and in love for Christ, then our work will be pleasing in the sight of God. When we just aren't sure what the best course of action is, we do well to remember what Paul wrote to the Philippians: "Do not be anxious about anything, but in everything, by prayer and petition, with thanksgiving, present your requests to God" (4:6).

> ***Topic 8:*** *Matthew 6:25-33: Therefore I tell you, do not worry about your life, what you will eat or drink; or about your body, what you will wear. Is not life more important than food, and the body more important than clothes? Look at the birds of the air; they do not sow or reap or store away in barns, and yet your heavenly Father feeds them. Are you not much more valuable than they? Who of you by worrying can add a single hour to his life? And why do you worry about clothes? See how the lilies of the field grow. They do not labor or spin. Yet I tell you that not even Solomon in all his splendor was dressed like one of these. If that is how God clothes the grass of the field, which is here today and tomorrow is thrown into the fire, will he not much more clothe you, O you of little faith? So do not worry, saying, "What shall we eat?" or "What shall we drink?" or "What shall we wear?" For the pagans run after all these things, and your heavenly Father knows that you need them. But seek first his kingdom and his righteousness, and all these things will be given to you as well.*
>
> *Philippians 4:19: My God will meet all your needs according to his glorious riches in Christ Jesus.*

When does human life begin? If you read *Roe versus Wade*, the infamous 1973 US Supreme Court decision that legalized abortion, you quickly realize that the court avoided this question. Over 30 years later, advances in biotechnology have pushed the question to the forefront of public debate in regard to the use of embryonic stem cells.

Stem cells are created immediately after an egg cell has been fertilized. "Human embryonic stem cells can develop into any of the body's 210 types of cells, a process that happens naturally during fetal development."[53] Scientists hope to grow tissue that can be used to help cure such diseases as Alzheimer's and cancer and to repair spinal cord injuries.

Most embryonic stem cells used in research come from embryos donated by private couples who have used the services of fertility clinics. A federal law prohibits spending federal dollars on tissue developed from human embryos. The law also prohibits using embryonic stem cells to grow other stem cells that in turn would be used to conduct research or to clone other embryos. President Clinton reinterpreted the original law to mean that federal money could be used for research if the embryos came from private donors. Under President Bush, the funding was again stopped.

Predictably, passions regarding embryonic stem cell research are running high. Abortion opponents consider the destruction of human embryos to be the same as killing unborn children. The president of the Family Research Council, Ken Connor, described embryonic stem cell research as "taking a human being and sacrificing it to the benefit of others."[54] Supporters of stem cell research have reached a different conclusion. One researcher said, "It's very unfortunate that those opposed to abortion are assuming that working with frozen embryos would be tantamount to killing a child. It's not like we're talking about a fetus or a baby. This is a science and health issue, a way to save thousands if not millions of lives. This is not an abortion issue."[55] The heart of the issue is the question, When does life begin? God has answered that question.

Advanced technology and the genetic revolution have raised other ethical questions that we have never had to answer before. One question has to do with the possibility of patenting life. In 1980 the US Supreme Court ruled in *Chakrabarty versus*

US that Ms. Chakrabarty's "genetically engineered microorganism designed to consume oil spills" could be patented.[56] The ruling reversed a long-standing view that "discoveries of nature" could not be patented.

This ruling raised the possibility that we may not own our own bodies. In a 1990 decision, the California Supreme Court found that a man did not actually own his own cells. John Moore had a rare form of cancer. While being treated at UCLA, a researcher discovered a protein in Moore's spleen that can be used to grow white blood cells, which are important anti-cancer agents. The university patented its find, which is now worth over $3 billion. When Moore sued for compensation, he was told that he had no ownership right to the patented cells.[57]

Questions to consider:

1. Should patents be granted for living organisms?

2. Should businesses be engaged in genetic research on stem cells, or is this best left to the government?

3. Should humankind be engaged in genetic research that has the potential to alter human beings?

Studies in genetics are advancing at a pace that would have seemed impossible just a few short years ago. The promise of new findings and the hope of new cures are exciting. Cures for cancer, Alzheimer's, Parkinson's, diabetes, and a host of other plagues seem within our grasp. But along with the benefits come some very real dangers. Some scientists have already pledged to clone a human being, despite scientific and government objections. Others predict that parents will soon be able to choose the traits they desire for their children.

Clearly this new knowledge poses some major ethical concerns.

These concerns underscore the need for the government, not the market, to dictate what will be considered acceptable.

Some people are all too willing to step beyond the bounds of proper ethical behavior for profit. Government regulations are needed to curb activities that demean life. As we discussed earlier in this book, in most cases the marketplace is the most efficient and effective way to allocate resources. However, human life is not a product that should be allocated by a market system. We have been created in the image of God and are his prize creation. The thought of producing made-to-order people is repugnant.

In the future, one of the most important roles of the government might be to regulate genetic research. The marketplace will not adequately safeguard human life. Finland allows doctors to euthanize the elderly and those afflicted with terminal illness. In this country, the state of Oregon has already passed an assisted suicide law. People seem willing to play God and to choose when to die or end life if the economic costs outweigh the benefits of living. Companies certainly would use the same standard. Driven by the profit motive, companies will soon supplant dignity, respect, and human life with the desire to make money. Until the market can adequately value life, it will be an inadequate system for governing genetic research.

This doesn't mean that Christians can't be involved in the business of genetic research. But we need to keep certain biblical principles in mind. We should never forget that God, not man, is the author of life. We know that God breathed the "breath of life" into Adam's nostrils, and he became a living person (Genesis 2:7). God then created Eve from one of Adam's ribs. Subsequent to that time, all life has begun at conception. The psalmist confirmed this when he wrote, "Surely I was sinful at birth, sinful from the time my mother conceived me" (Psalm 51:5). And God is not only the one who gives life, but he is also the only one who has the right to take life. Though in some situations he works through the agency of the government (Romans 13:4), our times are still in his hands (Psalm 31:15).

Human life has value also because God has redeemed us. Because God values us, we love and honor him. Christians show this by the good works we do and by placing our complete trust in God's grace and mercy. Because we know that we have value in Christ, we recognize that we have a purpose that is higher than simply trying to live the good life. Our purpose—and our desire—is to glorify God. We recognize that God has given us a set time on the earth to do this (Ecclesiastes 3).

It's important that we remember that the value of human life is found in Christ's redemption. If health, looks, intelligence, and earning potential are the standards by which we value life, we could very quickly find ourselves under the control of the market. The potential to manipulate human life is going to be a powerful motivator that will be hard to control. How much would you be willing to pay to eliminate the terminal cancer that will cut short your life? If it were possible to guarantee that your unborn child would not have Down's syndrome, would you pay the price? The mind is an incredible gift from God that is slowly destroyed by Alzheimer's disease. If you could buy a cure for a loved one, how much would it be worth? Nobody wants to see children suffer and die before they have the chance to experience much of life. Childhood leukemia, cystic fibrosis, and a host of other diseases cut short the promising lives of young children. Wouldn't we, as parents, pay as much as we could to make sure these afflictions don't harm our children?

Business stands to gain mightily by marketing such cures to desperate customers. We can easily imagine the intense demand that would develop for cures to horrific diseases that deprive people of dignity and life. Without much trouble, we can also imagine the abuses that could corrupt the system.

By patenting a cure, a firm would have a virtual monopoly and would be in position to dictate who lives and who dies. By controlling the supply in the face of intense demand, the price for life-preserving drugs would skyrocket in the marketplace. Corporate America would stand to earn handsome profits from the sale of life-saving drugs.

Allowing the marketplace to control the development of life-altering drugs and procedures introduces other potential problems. Again we can easily imagine how sinful people might use these discoveries. Cloning, aborting unborn babies with birth defects, euthanizing the elderly and dying, or altering genetic codes to dictate the traits a baby will possess are just the top of the slippery slope.

God owns life; we do not. The fact that we have the technical capability and the financial resources to design a potential life that meets our fancy does not mean that we should do it. Christians will want to use medical discoveries in ways that testify that God is the author of life. If corporate policies threaten to degrade God's gift of life in any way, Christian shareholders have an obligation to voice their concerns to management. Any shareholder who owns at least two hundred shares of a publicly traded firm on the New York Stock Exchange can file a shareholder resolution. These resolutions force management to address the issue by letting all shareholders vote on the issue. Likewise, Christian scientists and employees may want to think twice about working for firms that do not respect God's authority and creation. Through our actions, we can let a sinful world know that we do not condone its actions.

In the present business climate, working for policies that display respect for God may seem like a waste of effort. Imagine the ridicule a Christian would face if he or she would attempt to use a shareholder's resolution to stop a company from destroying human embryos for stem-cell research. Given the small chance of success and the huge risk to our egos, most of us would not even try. Or how many Christian employees are willing to sacrifice their careers in order to witness to their belief that God is the author of life? While we may not personally be responsible for the sinful actions of our employer, when do we speak up?

Job is an excellent role model for all Christians. Job was wealthy, "the greatest man among all the people of the East" (Job 1:3). Satan believed that he could get faithful Job to

renounce God if God would allow Satan to take aw
family and possessions. As Job's family, health, and
slipped away, the peer pressure to publicly reject God was
enormous. Not only did Job's friends urge him to abandon
God, but so did his wife. How easy it would have been at that
point for Job to follow popular opinion. Despite the lack of
support from his family and friends, Job remained faithful to
the Lord. As we see at the end of Job's story, God did not
abandon Job. Nor will God abandon us. Though we may feel
alone at the annual meeting or at the workplace, as the story of
Job so richly illustrates, that is not the case.

> **Topic 9:** *John 15:1-8: I am the true vine, and my Father is the gardener. He cuts off every branch in me that bears no fruit, while every branch that does bear fruit he prunes so that it will be even more fruitful. You are already clean because of the word I have spoken to you. Remain in me, and I will remain in you. No branch can bear fruit by itself; it must remain in the vine. Neither can you bear fruit unless you remain in me. I am the vine; you are the branches. If a man remains in me and I in him, he will bear much fruit; apart from me you can do nothing. If anyone does not remain in me, he is like a branch that is thrown away and withers; such branches are picked up, thrown into the fire and burned. If you remain in me and my words remain in you, ask whatever you wish, and it will be given you. This is to my Father's glory, that you bear much fruit, showing yourselves to be my disciples.*

In 2000, the chief financial officer of Wisconsin Energy earned a base salary of $407,500. Wisconsin Energy also gave him a salary guarantee that would protect his wage and benefit package for three years if he would lose his job because of a merger. The package also included a home repurchase agreement and the use of a company office and secretarial services for up to one year. Fifty other executives at Wisconsin Energy received similar packages.[58]

In the competitive marketplace, loss of jobs through mergers and restructuring are a way of life. However, companies don't generally treat all their employees like they do the key executives. In August of 1996, Pabst Brewing Company, the venerable beer company, announced that it was slashing health and death benefits for 770 union retirees and 43 nonunion retirees. The change was projected to save the company $3.5 million and to keep the company producing beer in Milwaukee.[59] The move was one of several steps Pabst took to try to reduce labor costs at its Milwaukee location. In the end it was still too little too late. In October of the same year, the company announced that it was closing its Milwaukee plant.

Pabst is not the only company that has looked to restructure benefit plans as a method of saving money. In 1997, Monsanto spun off the Solutia chemicals unit. Monsanto transferred the 16,000 retirees that worked in its unit to Solutia's care. The move immediately reduced Monsanto's health liability from $1.2 billion to $383 million. One year after the transfer, Solutia announced it was going to reduce the retirees' health-care benefits. The move saved Solutia $161 million.[60]

Questions to consider:

1. How far can a Christian go to restructure a labor relationship in order to save a business?

2. Is it right to treat executives differently than hourly employees when it comes to termination-benefit packages?

There are two legal ways to make more money in business. One is to sell more products or services. The other is to reduce costs.

Increasing sales is not easy. Think of the airline industry. Air travel has become a commodity in that it is hard to differentiate the services offered by different airlines. Cutting prices does not increase sales because fares are usually matched instantaneously by the competition. That is one reason airlines use frequent-flier programs. Since all airlines offer the same basic services, often with the same model planes, frequent-flier rewards are one way to differentiate companies from the competition and to build customer loyalty.

By cutting costs, a company can increase its profit without having to increase sales. Wal-Mart is an excellent example of a company that is almost religious about cost control. It is a major reason why Wal-Mart can maintain "everyday low prices." For example, if Wal-Mart spends $.90 out of every $1.00 in sales on expenses, the company earns $.10. If Kmart spends $.95 out of every $1.00 in sales on expenses, Kmart is earning only $.05 per dollar of sales. If Kmart wants to make the same amount of profit as Wal-Mart, it can either increase sales or decrease costs. To increase sales, it could cut its prices. Of course, reducing prices also reduces income if there isn't a corresponding reduction in costs. If Kmart reduces its prices, Wal-Mart can match Kmart's prices. But because of the greater profit margin Wal-Mart enjoys, it would beat Kmart at its own game. Cutting Kmart's internal costs is really the only strategy that will level the playing field between the two companies.

As the parable of the ten minas (Luke 19:11-26) makes clear, we are to be wise stewards of the resources God has entrusted to us. Cutting costs is a good stewardship strategy. But it's a strategy most business students fail to appreciate. The members of my strategic management class used a computer simulation that allowed them to form their own companies. They then used the interactive simulation to compete with one another. The company that earned the most money at the end of the semester was the winner. Almost every team initially spent large amounts of money on advertising and marketing programs to build sales. By the end of the semester, the advertising budgets were reduced, and most of the money was going into programs to reduce production costs.

Cutting costs poses an ethical challenge to Christians. When we promise to provide retirement benefits, health-care benefits, or anything else for our employees, it is not right to break these promises. The Lord takes promises very seriously:

"When a man makes a vow to the LORD or takes an oath to obligate himself by a pledge, he must not break his word but must do everything he said" (Numbers 30:2). In the case of Pabst, however, economic conditions seemed to justify the decision. But God doesn't list "economic conditions" as a valid reason or excuse for breaking our word. Nehemiah did not allow economic considerations to interfere with his demand that the people promise to stop engaging in unethical business practices (Nehemiah 5:12,13). If Pabst needed to alter its agreement with retirees, the least the company could have done was renegotiate the terms instead of unilaterally stopping the payments.

The Monsanto case involved a rather deceitful effort to deprive employees of benefits that they had been promised. It makes no difference whether Monsanto or the new firm eliminated the benefits. The interest of the employees appears to have been sacrificed in the name of the bottom line. If the goal is to reduce costs, the company needs to be honest and tell the employees up front.

This case study started with the discussion of the benefit packages given to executives at Wisconsin Electric. Executive compensation has become a hot topic in recent years. Many people feel that executives are overcompensated for the services they provide. Others feel that it is unfair that such a large pay gap exists between executives and average-wage earners. Some even argue that the law should fix a ratio between executive salaries and those earned by the lowest paid hourly employees.

While such proposals have some merit and come with good intentions, I believe that they are misguided. Scripture recognizes that people have been blessed with different gifts and talents. Paul's analogy of the body is applicable to business. The CEO may be the brain, but without the hands, feet, and eyes, where would he or she be? Similarly, without someone guiding the actions of the hands, feet, and eyes, how can the organization be successful? The economic system acknowledges the differences in people by setting wages according to the supply of, and demand for, various talents. As Christians, we will certainly not want to exploit people or deprive them of their justly earned wages. However, people certainly are not entitled to anything more than that to which they agreed. In Philippians 4:12 Paul reminds us that we are to be content with what we have.

> **Topic 10:** *Proverbs 3:7-9: Do not be wise in your own eyes; fear the Lord and shun evil. This will bring health to your body and nourishment to your bones. Honor the Lord with your wealth, with the firstfruits of all your crops.*

CBS has captured the nation's attention with its popular series *Survivor*. On the show, people are divided into groups and placed in remote places or deserted islands. Each week a person is voted off until only one remains. That person wins $1 million.

Not to be outdone, FOX created *Temptation Island*. Four unmarried couples were placed on a deserted island. The men lived on one side of the island; the women lived on the other. To keep viewers interested, the men were surrounded by beautiful women while the women were entertained by male models. Producers suggested that the show would test the strength of each couple's relationship.[61] But the rest of the world soon figured out that the premise was to see which person would be first to give in to lust and cheat on his or her partner.

Questions to consider:

1. How far should business go to make a profit?

2. How involved should a Christian employee get when the employer's business project appears to contradict God's commands?

We previously defined *allocative efficiency* as "the combination of goods and services that satisfies society's material wants." We also argued that a market economy is the best way to achieve that allocation of products and services. While capitalism may be the most efficient way to satisfy our wants and desires, it doesn't offer a mechanism to control demands that aren't God pleasing. A show like *Temptation Island* is a case in point. People may demand immorality. That doesn't mean that we should provide it.

Economic systems don't express morality. The producers and consuming public provide that dimension. Christian businesses have to swim against the tide because our morality is not compatible with that of society. This poses an obvious danger for the Christians in business. If the only way to stay in business is to cater to the base instincts of a corrupt and sinful world, what are we to do? Should Christians invest in companies that provide products or services that are not compatible with our religious beliefs?

I posed this question to my Business Ethics class. One individual spent quite a bit of time trying to devise a system to rank companies based on the degree of immorality associated with their products. For example, investing in Playboy Enterprises was classified as definitely wrong, but Phillip Morris was acceptable because the Kraft food division offset the tobacco and alcohol sales. The class rejected the system.

Napster posed another problem for the class. Napster was a service that allowed the user to download copyrighted music for free. When I asked if this was stealing, many students went to great lengths to justify their own personal use of the service. In the end, the class split between two alternative investing plans. One plan suggested that Christians could invest in almost any company because they would then have a better chance of changing the policies of that company. The other claimed that Christians should not invest at all in those companies that are openly hostile to our Christian beliefs.

I mention investing because most of us have 401(k) or 403b retirement plans that make investments in a variety of companies. As long as the returns are good, we blissfully ignore the moral values of the companies that are making us money. But our private investments pose questions similar to those that Christian businesspeople confront every day. How far do you go to make a dollar?

The television and motion picture industries are examples of industries that go to great lengths to give people what they want. Remember the *Rocky* movies starring Sylvester Stallone? There was *Rocky, Rocky II, Rocky III,* and who cares how many others. When Hollywood finds a successful horse, it will be ridden until it is dead. This approach often leads to one-upmanship. We get movies that are gorier, bloodier, and more violent, or that expose more skin, than the competition. In the process, the audience becomes desensitized to what it sees. We end up with a culture that has no attention span and in which everything goes.

In this culture, the First Commandment gets lost in the competition to earn a dollar. And we so easily justify following the world in order to earn our living.

In the classroom, students are quick to say what they would or would not do if confronted with an ethical decision at work. But, in reality, the answers don't come so easily. For example, I suspect that few of us would schedule a show like *Temptation Island* if we owned the network. But what would our decision be if we worked for the network and were ordered by our boss to schedule the show? Just to make the example interesting, let us assume that we make $200,000 per year, enjoy six weeks of paid vacation, and are just one year from retirement. Would we sacrifice our jobs and refuse to schedule the show?

It is easy to sit in a classroom or read a book secure in the knowledge that this is only a "what if" game. In the end, we lose nothing if we say we would quit the company. In reality, some people have a lot to lose, however.

I think of my last boss. I don't know if he was a Christian. I do know that he was 50 years old and that he had worked in retail all of his adult life. Within the company he was known as a golden boy, meaning that he was on the fast track to an executive position in the home office. Then the unexpected happened. Our CEO committed suicide, and a new management team was hired. Suddenly, my boss was no longer on the fast track to success. He told me how afraid he was of being fired. As he put it, discount retailing is a young man's business, and he was too old to start

141

over. If he got fired, he would not be able to get another job comparable to the one he then enjoyed.

Losing material comforts would be hard to accept. But for Christians, our greater concern is eternal life. The parable of the rich fool (Luke 12:15-21) tells us what will happen if we trust in our own talents for security and success. God's command is clear, "Fear the Lord your God, serve him only" (Deuteronomy 6:13). Jesus' words also encourage us not to fear the consequences. He tells us to seek first his kingdom and righteousness, trusting that he will take care of the rest.

All Christians engaged in business can take comfort in the story of Abraham's wife, Sarah, which is recorded in Genesis 18. When God ordered Abraham to move to a foreign land, Sarah went with him. Imagine what she gave up by moving to that new land. Sarah traded her support system of family and friends for an uncertain future in an unknown land. But Sarah feared God and accompanied her husband. Sarah later realized the fulfillment of God's plan for her. She became a mother in her old age. Her son was the forefather of the Savior of the world.

We too can follow God's plan, even when we travel in unknown and frightening territory. We know that God will be with us and that his plan for us may be better than anything we could imagine.

> **Topic 11:** *James 1:5-8: If any of you lacks wisdom, he should ask God, who gives generously to all without finding fault, and it will be given to him. But when he asks, he must believe and not doubt, because he who doubts is like a wave of the sea, blown and tossed by the wind. That man should not think he will receive anything from the Lord; he is a double-minded man, unstable in all he does.*

Does trusting in God make good business sense?

Johns Manville was an industry leader in the manufacturing of building materials. The company promoted the use of asbestos as a fire retardant and insulator. It was used extensively in public buildings, such as schools. The problem with asbestos, as Johns Manville officials well knew, was that it posed a danger to human health. Prolonged exposure caused lung disease. But instead of admitting the danger early on, company officials repeatedly denied the problem, assuring everyone that the product was safe.

In 1974, five hundred men who had used the material while building ships during WWII filed the first class action lawsuit against Johns Manville. By 1982, more than 4,000 asbestos-related cases had been settled by the company, while 17,000 more were still pending.[62] No one had any idea how many claims could eventually be filed because the disease caused by inhaling asbestos fibers could take years to develop.

On August 26, 1982, the company filed for protection under chapter 11 of the Bankruptcy Code. All claims against the company were effectively stopped, even though the company was not insolvent. To some it looked like Johns Manville was using the Bankruptcy Code to avoid responsibility.

In 1984, the US Supreme Court, in a 5-4 decision, ruled that management could renege on a labor contract once it filed a bankruptcy petition. "The company must show that the pacts are a burden and that a variety of factors 'balance' in favor of rejecting the agreements."[63] The decision allowed companies to avoid paying the wages previously agreed to in a collectively bargained labor contract. By rejecting the labor contract in bankruptcy court, the company could unilaterally impose a lower wage rate or benefit package on the employees. Continental Airlines was a direct beneficiary of that ruling. Some charged that Continental was using the courts to break labor contracts.[64]

In Wisconsin, activist groups representing the labor force had an additional concern regarding bankruptcy. The activists targeted FirstBank in Milwaukee for a possible boycott. The groups were upset that FirstBank, along with other Wisconsin banks, lobbied to have Wisconsin bankruptcy laws changed. The change would have given secured creditors preference over wage liens if an employer would go bankrupt. This means that when the firm would be liquidated, any proceeds would be used to pay creditors before employees. The activists perceived this move as being antilabor.[65]

Questions to consider:

1. Should the bankruptcy code be used to unilaterally terminate collective bargaining agreeements?

2. When is it proper for a Christian to use the Bankruptcy Code for protection from creditors?

The right to petition for bankruptcy relief is embedded in Article I, Section 8, of the United States Constitution. Just what form of relief should be granted has been the source of political controversy throughout the years. The goal of the bankruptcy law is to allow debtors a new start while protecting the rights of creditors. If bankruptcy laws provide too much protection for debtors, creditors will be leery of extending credit to consumers, fearing that they will never collect. If the law is slanted too much in favor of creditors, debtors will not be able to start over and may never be able to repay their debts. Early versions of the bankruptcy law favored creditors over debtors. In 1978, the Bankruptcy Reform Act swung the pendulum in favor of debtors. Current revisions suggested by Congress once again seem to favor creditors.

Bankruptcy protection becomes an ethical issue when it is used for the wrong purpose. In the case of Johns Manville, the company had been aware of the dangerous health risks posed by prolonged exposure to asbestos but did nothing about it. Instead, the company went about its business as if nothing were wrong. Even insurance companies were aware of the dangers of asbestos. "By 1981, many of the nation's insurers had known for decades that asbestos workers were dying early, but kept silent while their underwriters wrote policies for workmen's compensation and comprehensive general liability as fast as they could put pencil to paper."[66] When the lawsuits started to mount and Johns Manville's legal defense started to crumble, company executives turned to the Bankruptcy Code for protection.

Filing for bankruptcy with the intent to escape poor business decisions is similar to stealing. Johns Manville was not in financial trouble. The market for its products had not evaporated. Competition had not taken its customers. The government had not passed any laws that ruined the company's business. Instead, Johns Manville was in bankruptcy court because of its own greedy, self-serving, shortsighted business strategy. Instead of dealing with the issue when it first surfaced, Johns Manville went about business as usual with no concern for the health of its workers. It earned profits while its employees were exposed to a known health hazard, got sick, and died. Only when Johns Manville's own employees demanded justice did Johns Manville look for protection.

When the courts accepted Johns Manville's bankruptcy petition, two things happened. First, all claims against the company were frozen. Second, the company was allowed to reorganize and avoid future liability. Creditors and employees were outraged that Johns Manville was going to be allowed to escape the ramifications of its past decisions. The judge ruled that "in the instant case, not only would liquidation be wasteful and inefficient in destroying the utility of valuable assets of the companies as well as jobs, but, more importantly, liquidation would preclude just compensation of some present asbestos victims and all future asbestos claimants."[67]

The bankruptcy judge made a good point. If the company were destroyed, those who might have future claims for asbestos-related injuries would be unable to collect. Under the reorganization plan, some money was to be set aside to compensate those people. The compensation probably wouldn't be as high as the victims might hope, but at least they would receive some compensation. Though this is a compelling argument, it fails to take into account the gravity of Johns Manville's actions. Johns Manville was allowed to escape debts that it had incurred and had been obligated to pay as a result of its business practices. That is stealing. By filing for bankruptcy, it was in effect profiting from a tool that the government established to help those who are down on their luck. Stupidity and greed should not be protected. By using the law for the personal gain of the company, Johns Manville stole from its creditors.

It could be further argued that Johns Manville was guilty of breaking the Fifth Commandment. The company allowed people to be exposed to an agent that it knew would kill them. "Do not do anything that endangers your neighbor's life. I am the LORD" (Leviticus 19:16). By manufacturing a product they knew was harmful, Johns Manville executives demonstrated their ignorance of God's will. Christian businesspeople are morally obligated to protect those who use their products. By its negligence, Johns Manville, in effect, killed its consumers.

Since that time, other companies have used the bankruptcy courts to escape the consequences of their poor business decisions. In 1981, AH Robins filed for bankruptcy as a result of legal liability stemming from its intrauterine contraceptive device known as the Dalkon Shield. AH Robins knew that the device had a failure rate nearly five times higher than what they advertised. To make matters worse, the longer the device was kept in the body, the more likely it was to cause infection and health problems for a woman. The product was sold in the United States from 1971 to 1974, but AH Robins knew about the health risks as early as 1970. It did nothing to stop the harm.

In 1995, Dow Corning filed for bankruptcy protection from lawsuits stemming from the sale of its breast implants.

The list of companies doing this continues to grow. The point is that companies seem quite willing to use the law to escape the consequences of their actions.

The higher road, the road we hope Christians take, would be to think about our actions and take responsibility for them. The law should not be a strategic management tool used to further the interest of our business. If taking responsibility for our actions means going out of business, so be it.

The lobbying effort by FirstBank poses an interesting problem for Christians in the banking industry, although the problem may not be readily apparent. We know from Scripture that employees are entitled to their wages. Scripture also suggests that if a debt to a fellow Christian goes unpaid, the Christian creditor should forgive it. Though, with the second principle, the Scriptures are speaking about a business relationship between two Christians, it still provides food for thought when considering bankruptcy proceedings. On the basis of those two principles, I have a feeling that in a bankruptcy proceeding, the payment of employee wages should take precedence over repayment of loans. In many cases, the employees are the ones who can least afford to be deprived of what they are owed. The important point is that even in a seemingly mundane and technical rule change, Christians are confronted with ethical dilemmas.

ELEVEN

WHAT does this mean?

"Whatever you do, whether in word or deed, do it all in the name of the Lord Jesus, giving thanks to God the Father through him."—Apostle Paul (Colossians 3:17)

Many of us feel ill at ease as we try to determine how our Christian faith will reflect itself in the workplace. Through countless sermons, we have been told that greed, materialism, and an unhealthy focus on our own personal well-being are sinful forces that are undermining our society. It doesn't take a rocket scientist to recognize that business contributes to the problem. We have all seen marketing campaigns, heavy on sex appeal, that promote instantaneous gratification and suggest very brazenly that we deserve whatever is being sold. Such business practices are convenient targets that are easy to identify and condemn. Unfortunately, some other objectionable business practices are not even questioned. Charging astronomically high interest rates on short-term loans, targeting the elderly with sophisticated marketing techniques, and using the courts to avoid legal liability are accepted practices that raise serious ethical issues for Christians.

The way business is conducted in a society is shaped by the economic system that is in place. In America, capitalism dictates that a competitive market composed of rational individuals will allocate resources through the pricing mechanism. In other words, supply and demand rules. Consumers will make their preferences known through purchases made in the marketplace. Suppliers will try to satisfy consumer demand by producing and selling products in that same marketplace. The competition among buyers, sellers, and one another will theoretically result in maximum selection at the lowest possible price.

We can't excuse ourselves if we try to hide behind the pretext of economic competition to justify business practices that go against God's will. A capitalist economic system is not to blame for our sinful practices.

Scripture does not prohibit Christians from making money in the marketplace. Bill Gates, the founder of Microsoft, made a fortune while his computer operating system helped make businesses more efficient.

Looking out for our own self-interests does not automatically imply greed. Faced with intense competition and an eroding market share, executives at Master Lock could either move production to Mexico or go out of business. That is not much of a choice.

Finally, Christ did not warn people that they would lose their souls if they became rich. America has been blessed with one of the most productive economies the world has ever seen. We do not have to become Mennonites and shun worldly possessions to please God. We do have to guard against jeopardizing our salvation, against allowing trust in our own abilities or material possessions to become more important than our relationship with God.

The lesson for us, as Christians in the world of business, is not to flee from the marketplace but to learn how to apply our faith in ways that will help others discover God's promise for them. That does not mean we should force our views down the throats of our colleagues. That would probably be illegal as well as unproductive. But by conducting our business affairs in a God-pleasing manner, the world will see that we are different. Through our example, others may be led to think of their relationship with God.

At a Bible study on business ethics, one person argued that we need to be careful about expecting to use business as a tool to promote Christianity. This person pointed out that it is the mission of the church to spread the gospel message. The responsibility of Christians is to witness to those around us and to set an example by the lives we lead. According to this person, just as the government has power over secular but not spiritual matters, we cannot expect business to spread the gospel message.

While this individual had a point, we must not divorce ourselves from the faith that we so dearly hold. Granted, we should not expect, nor should we want, GM or Microsoft to promote a particular religion. That isn't its function. But we remember that business organizations are human-made creations. The Nobel laureate Milton Friedman was correct when he observed that corporations are incapable of doing good or bad. Only people can make decisions, have responsibilities, or act in a humane or reckless fashion. The corporation, as an artificial entity, simply reflects the will of those who operate through it.

Because we, as individuals, can shape the corporation, the way we live our lives can have an influence on the corporate culture. Because we live in a sinful world, we don't expect that this will be an easy row to hoe. A Christian would not tolerate cheating or stealing by a fellow employee as an acceptable form of behavior. But what will the Christian do when the corporation itself engages in these behaviors? As we have seen previously, marketing campaigns and the use of bankruptcy laws and employment policies can all fall short of what is right and God pleasing. As Christian employees, what do we do about it? When an individual is 50 years old, has six weeks of vacation every year, and is making six figures, taking a stand against established business practices is not easy. Much is at stake in terms of money and status. How the Christian handles those dilemmas has to be a matter of individual prayer and reflection. But compromising with God is not a matter of individual choice. The minute we put our interest or well-being in front of God's will, we have not only chosen the wrong ethical path to follow, but we have sinned.

When I started this book, I was looking for firm answers to ethical problems that face businesspeople. I wanted to be able to point to specific Bible passages that would clearly delineate what was right and what was wrong. I did not find what I was looking for. Instead, I now realize that Christians in business need to search Scripture and pray for the wisdom to answer hard questions.

A Christian approach to business ethics is akin to peeling an onion. As we take off one layer, another appears. As we dig deeper into the Lord's Word, we begin to realize that our ethical questions are more complicated than we care to admit. At the same time, we also understand even more clearly that as redeemed children of God, we want all of our lives and actions to give glory to God. In the end, there are no cookie-cutter answers to any given problem. Each Christian needs to diligently examine the motives behind the decision, search Scripture, and pray for the guidance that God is sure to provide. Because we have the privilege of being called God's children, Christian businesspeople will be satisfied with nothing less.

ENDNOTES

Chapter One

[1] Savage, Mark. "Master Lock Employees Squeezed between Costs and Profits. Some Workers Doubt Need to Move Work South, Are Unhappy with Union," *Milwaukee Journal Sentinel.* September 26, 1999, 3.

[2] Hawkins, Lee. "Key to a Turnaround." *Milwaukee Journal Sentinel.* August 28, 2000, 150.

[3] Bureau of Labor Market Information and Customer Services. "Milwaukee County Workforce Profile." Wisconsin Department of Workforce Development, December 2000, 6.

[4] Ibid.

[5] "Minorities as Percent of Total Population by Community." *Milwaukee Journal Sentinel.*

[6] Office of Economic Advisors. "2000–2001. Affirmative Action for Milwaukee County," Wisconsin Department of Workforce Development.

[7] Holzer, Harry J. "Career Advancement Prospects and Strategies for Low-Wage Minority Workers." *Low-Wage Workers in the New Economy.* Edited by Kazis and Miller. Washington DC: The Urban Institute Press, March 1, 2000, 224-226.

[8] Rust, Joel. "Transportation Equity and Access to Jobs," UW-Milwaukee Center for Economic Development, 2004, 30.

[9] "1999 Residential Sales: District 17." Assessor's Office.

[10] Borsuk, Alan J. "Kids May Pay for City's High Rate of Single Moms." *Milwaukee Journal Sentinel.* July 3, 2002, 1A.

[11] Griffin, Kawanza L. "City Ranks Poorly on Teen Births." *Milwaukee Journal Sentinel.* January 26, 2003, 2B.

[12] US Census Bureau. "County Estimates for People of All Ages in Poverty for Wisconsin: 1997."

[13] US Census Bureau. "State and County Quick Facts: Milwaukee County, Wisconsin." Washington DC: US Government Printing Office, 2004.

[14] Wisconsin Department of Public Instruction. "2000-2001 Graduation Final Publication Report."

[15] Milwaukee Board of Fire and Police Commissioners. "City of Milwaukee 2001 Public Safety Report."

[16] Millman, Joel. "Fortune Brands Moves Units to Mexico to Lower Costs—Some of America's Most Recognized Products Are Made South of the Border." *The Wall Street Journal*. August 7, 2001, B2.

[17] Ibid.

[18] Ibid.

Chapter Two

[1] National Agricultural Statistics Service. "Wisconsin: Farm Numbers and Land in Farms."

[2] Ross, Michael E. "It Seemed Like a Good Idea at the Time."

[3] Muhm, Don. *The NFO: A Farm Belt Rebel: The History of the National Farmers Organization*. Rochester, MN: Lone Oak Press, 2000.

[4] Olmstead, Alan, and Paul W. Rhode. "The Transformation of Northern Agriculture, 1910–1990." Edited by Engerman and Gallman. *The Cambridge Economic History of the United States*. Vol. 3, Cambridge: Cambridge University Press, 2001, 701.

[5] Smith, Rebecca. "Power Deregulation—A Year Later: Most Players Think New System Works." *San Francisco Chronicle*. March 31, 1999, B1.

[6] Hauter, Wenonah, and Tyson Slocum. "It's Greed Stupid! Debunking the Ten Myths of Utility Deregulation." *Public Citizen Critical Mass Energy and Environment Program.* January 2001, 4.

[7] *Frontline*, "Blackout." PBS, June 2001. Available at www.pbs.org/wgbh/pages/frontline/shows/blackout/.

[8] Berthelsen, Christian. "How Energy Giant Tried to Cut a Deal: Duke Inc. Offered to Reduce Bill If State Halted Probes." *San Francisco Chronicle.* May 3, 2001, A4.

[9] Ibid.

[10] Ibid.

[11] Bustillo, Miguel, Tim Reiterman, and Mitchell Landsberg, "California and the West; The California Energy Crisis; Capitol Blame Game Frays Bipartisanship; GOP lawmakers criticize PUC at Assemble Hearing; The Party Plans Radio Ads Attacking Governor. Democrats Target Past Republican Leaders." *Los Angeles Times.* February 8, 2001, A3.

[12] Hauter, 9.

[13] Ibid.

Chapter Three

[1] Romell, Rick. "Big Investor Seeks Change for Gehl: Florida Man Urges West Bend Firm to Sell Farm Equipment Division." *Milwaukee Journal Sentinel.* June 12, 1997, 1.

[2] Sorking, Andrew Ross. "Putting 'Hostile' Back into Takeover." *New York Times.* February 25, 2001, BU1.

[3] Romell.

[4] Slavin, Stephen L. *Macroeconomics.* 4th edition. Chicago: Irwin, 1996, 73.

[5] "Exxon, Toyota, GM to Join on Fuel Cell." *Milwaukee Journal Sentinel.* January 2, 2001, 1D.

[6] Federal Trade Commission. "FTC Issues Report on Midwest Gasoline Price Investigation." March 30, 2001.

[7] Aron, Leon. "The Death of Soviet Control." *The American Enterprise,* 11 (1): 38.

[8] Ibid.

[9] Gross Domestic Product (GDP) is the total market value of all final goods and services produced by a country in one year.

[10] Elliott, John E. "Disintegration of the Soviet Politico-Economic System." *International Journal of Social Economics.* 22 (3): 31.

[11] Ibid.

[12] Aron.

[13] The Average American home is approximately 2,300 square feet, and the family size was estimated to be three. Nine square meters is approximately 81 square feet.

[14] Aron.

[15] Aron.

[16] Kudrov, Valentin. "The Comparison of the USSR and USA Economies by IMEMO in the 1970's." *Europe-Asia Studies.* 49 (5): 883.

[17] Aron.

[18] Aron.

[19] Tokic, Damir. "What Went Wrong with the Dot-Coms?" *Journal of Investing.* 11 (2): 52–57.

[20] Rose, Craig D. "Only a Few Bad Apples? Despite Reforms, Investors Haven't Seen the Last of Corporate Greed." *San Diego Union-Tribune.* May 4, 2003, H1.

[21] Smith, Adam. *An Inquiry into the Nature and Causes of the Wealth of Nations.* New York: The Modern Library, 1937, 14.

[22] Ibid, 423.

[23] Ibid, 81.

[24] Ibid, 79.

[25] Smith, Adam. *The Theory of Moral Sentiments.* Indianapolis: Liberty Classics, 1976, 276.

[26] Ibid, 423.

[27] Ibid, 71.

[28] Smith, Adam. *An Inquiry into the Nature and Causes of the Wealth of Nations.* 747.

[29] Smith, Adam. *The Theory of Moral Sentiments.* 159.

[30] Bureau of Labor Statistics. "Consumer Expenditure in 1999," US Department of Labor, 8.

[31] Office of Management and Budget. "Table 22-1. Budget Authority by Function, Category, and Program FY2002."

[32] International Labor Office. "Every Child Counts: New Estimates on Child Labor." Geneva, Switzerland: International Labor Organization, 2002, 23.

[33] Ibid, 33.

[34] Bachman, S. L. "The Political Economy of Child Labor and Its Impacts on International Business." *Business Economics.* 35 (3): 32.

Chapter Four

[1] Theiberger, Frederic. *King Solomon.* London: Horowitz Publishing, 1947, 213.

[2] Kuske, David, *Luther's Catechism.* Milwaukee: Northwestern Publishing House, 1998, 4.

[3]Schlosser, Eric. "The Business of Pornography: Most of the Outsize Profits Being Generated by Pornography Today Are Being Earned by Businesses Not Traditionally Associated with the Sex Industry," *US News and World Report*. 42 (9): 42-51.

[4]Office of National Drug Control Policy. *The Economic Costs of Drug Abuse in the United States*. Washington, DC: Executive Office of the President, No. NCJ-190636, 5.

[5]Office of National Drug Control Policy. "National Drug Control Strategy Executive Summary, Fiscal Year 2002." Washington, DC: Executive Office of the President, 1.

[6]Ecumenical Task Force of the Niagara Frontier. "Background on the Love Canal," University Archives, University Libraries, State University of New York at Buffalo.

[7]Boyes, William, and Michael Melvin. *Economics*. Boston: Houghton Mifflin Co., 1999, 687.

[8]Ibid, 816.

Chapter Five

[1]Pabst, Georgia. "Purple Passions: Colorful Building Angers Some Business Neighbors." *Milwaukee Journal Sentinel*. January 7, 2001, 1B.

[2]Boyes, 821.

[3]Kay, John. "Staking a Moral Claim (Proposal for a Social Market Perspective on Economics)." *New Statesmen*. 125 (4305): 19.

Chapter Six

[1]Kaye, H. Stephen. "Improved Employment Opportunities for People with Disabilities." Washington, DC: National Institute on Disability and Rehabilitation Research, 2003, 21.

[2]Ibid.

[3] McNeil, John. "Disability." Washington, DC: US Census Bureau, 2001.

[4] Administration for Children and Families. "ACF News and Facts." Washington, DC: US Department of Health and Human Services, 2001.

[5] Rector, Robert. "The Effects of Welfare Reform." *Heritage Foundation*. March 15, 2001.

[6] Aquinas, Thomas. *Summa of the Summa*. Edited and annotated by Peter Kreeft. San Francisco: Ignatius Press, 1990, 391.

[7] Chatterjee, Sumana, and Raghavan Sudarsan. "Bitter Trail: Who's Responsible for Labor Atrocities?" *Milwaukee Journal Sentinel*. June 23, 2001, 8D.

[8] Ibid, 12A.

[9] US Census Bureau. "Income, Poverty, and Health Insurance Coverage in the United States 2003." Washington, DC: US Government Printing Office, 2004, 9.

[10] Ibid, 14.

[11] Ceniceros, Roberto. "Employers, Health Plans Trying Various Remedies for Soaring Drug Costs." *Business Insurance*. 37 (26) :4.

[12] US Conference of Catholic Bishops. "Economic Justice for All: Catholic Social Teaching and the US Economy." *National Catholic Reporter*. January 9, 1987, 10.

[13] Ibid, 11.

[14] Chewning, Richard. *Biblical Principles and Economics: The Foundations*. Colorado Springs: NavPress Publishing, 1990, 130.

[15] Sacks, Jonathan. "Markets and Morals." *First Things: The Journal of Religion, Culture, and Public Life*. August 2000, 23.

Chapter Seven

[1] Hoffman, W. Michael, Robert E. Frederick, and Mark S. Schwartz, eds. *Business Ethics: Readings and Cases in Corporate Morality.* Boston: McGraw-Hill, 2000, 1.

[2] Ibid, 2.

[3] Ibid, 89.

[4] Deutsch, Anthony. "Mercy Killings." *Milwaukee Journal Sentinel.* April 11, 2001, 5A.

[5] Reich, Robert. "The New Meaning of Corporate Social Responsibility." *California Management Review.* Winter 1998: 8-18.

[6] Ellwanger, Joseph W. "Partnership Registry Good for City." *Milwaukee Journal Sentinel.* Letter to the Editor. July 11, 1999.

[7] Reich, 9.

Chapter Eight

[1] Hartman, Laura P., ed. *Perspectives in Business Ethics.* Boston: McGraw-Hill, 1998, 91-99.

[2] www.Amazon.com. Subject: ethics. Accessed in March 2005.

[3] Lawrence, Anne T., James E. Post, and James Weber. *Business and Society: Stakeholders, Ethics, Public Policy.* Boston: McGraw-Hill, 1999, 58.

[4] Reich, 2.

[5] Chewning, 278.

[6] Post, Lawrence, and Weber. 60, 61.

[7] Post, 59.

[8] General Motors Corporation. "2003 Annual Report." 4.

[9] Joint Committee on Legislative Organization. "Highlights of State and Local Finance in Wisconsin." *Wisconsin Bluebook.* Madison: Legislative Reference Bureau, 2005, 828.

[10] Post, 59.

[11] Di Norcia, Vincent. *Hard Like Water: Ethics in Business.* Toronto: Oxford University Press, 1999, 36.

[12] Hartman, 246.

[13] Hartman, 270–273.

[14] Nixon, Robert. "Students Protest 'Sweatshops' Outside of Kohls." *Westchester County Business Journal,* October 23, 2000, 8.

[15] Miller, D.W. "Sweatshop Protest Ends at U of Michigan. *The Chronicle of Higher Education.* 45 (30): April 2, 1999.

[16] "Millennium 2000: Environment." Television program aired January 2, 2000, 11:23 A.M. ET. Available at www.cnn.com/TRANSCRIPTS/0001/02/se.35.html.

[17] Post, 59.

[18] Unger, Ray. "Anatomy of a Stock Market Hiccup." *The Capital Times.* November 4, 1997, 1C.

[19] Norris, Floyd. "Auditors Have a Responsibility to Call Sham Profits What They Are." *Milwaukee Journal Sentinel.* May 20, 2001, 3D.

[20] AG Edwards Inc. "Annual Report Fiscal Year 2001," 39.

[21] Norris.

Chapter Nine

[1] Brandt, Walther I. ed. *Luther's Works.* Philadelphia: Muhlenberg Press, 1962, 247.

[2] Ibid, 251.

[3] Ibid, 248.

[4] Ibid, 258.

[5] Ibid, 295.

[6] Ibid, 290.

[7] Ibid, 296.

[8] Ibid, 300.

[9] Ibid, 276.

[10] Ibid, 249.

[11] Ibid, 265.

[12] Ibid, 270-271.

[13] Ibid, 286.

Chapter Ten

[1] Michele, Tom. "Impact of Proposed Crandon Mine Explained." *Rhinelander Daily News.* April 4, 1995, 1.

[2] Wisconsin Department of Revenue. "Wisconsin Adjusted Gross Income by County, 1991-1995." *Wisconsin Bluebook.* Madison, WI: Legislative Reference Bureau, 649.

[3] Wisconsin Department of Workforce Development. "Forest County Workforce Profile." Division of Workforce Excellence, Bureau of Workforce Information, July 1999, 6.

[4] US Census Bureau. "USA Counties 1998—Poverty: Forest County Wisconsin."

[5] Behm, Don, Alan Borusk, and Lee Hawkins. "Mining Proposal Gets Cold Reception across State in Green Bay, Milwaukee, Foes Say Mine Could Hurt Environment." *Milwaukee Journal Sentinel.* February 18, 1997, 1.

[6] Millard, Johnson. "The Checks and Balances in Pursuing the Crandon Mine." *Corporate Report Wisconsin*. August 1, 1997, S14.

[7] Flasch, Jim. "The Crandon Mine and Northeast WI." *Marketplace Magazine*. December 10, 1996, 30.

[8] Vanden Brook, Tom. "Company Developing Crandon Mine Offers New Environmental Safeguards." *Milwaukee Journal Sentinel*. December 9, 1998, 1.

[9] Ibid.

[10] Millard.

[11] Millard.

[12] Vanden Brook.

[13] Ibid.

[14] Congress, Senate, Governmental Affairs Committee. "Senate Subcommittee Hearings on Sweepstakes." 106th Congress, 1st Session, March 10, 1999.

[15] Zahn, Mary. "Waiting for a Check That Doesn't Arrive: Elderly Sure That They Had Won End Up Drained of Cash, Dreams Swept Up in Sweepstakes. First in two parts." *Milwaukee Journal Sentinel*. March 14, 1999, 1.

[16] Jones, Meg. "State's Sweepstakes Trial Gets Under Way." *Milwaukee Journal Sentinel*. November 1, 2000, 1B.

[17] Zahn.

[18] Jones.

[19] Holland.

[20] Ibid.

[21] Adams, David M., and Edward L. Maine. *Business Ethics for the 21st Century*. Mayfield: Mountain View, 1998, 355.

[22] www.ftc.gov.

[23] Borowski, Greg. "Council OKs Lead Paint Lawsuit." *Milwaukee Journal Sentinel.* October 19, 2000, 1B.

[24] Ibid.

[25] Yue Jones, Terril. "Ford, Firestone 'Insane.'" *Milwaukee Journal Sentinel.* May 28, 2001, 10.

[26] Hajewski, Doris. "The Unsettling Price of Low-Cost Clothes." *Milwaukee Journal Sentinel.* December 29, 2000, 11A.

[27] Ibid, 1A.

[28] Ibid, 4L.

[29] Ibid, 12A.

[30] Ibid, 10A.

[31] Ibid, 12D.

[32] Sabo, Congressman Martin. "How Uncle Sam Could Help to Address the Income Gap."

[33] Lester, Will. "Economic Divide Growing, Poll Finds Many Feel." *Milwaukee Journal Sentinel.* June 22, 2001, 9A.

[34] Wiseman, Michael. "In Midst of Reform: Wisconsin 1997." *The Urban Institute,* 1999, 4.

[35] Ibid, 8.

[36] Department of Workforce Development. "Wisconsin Works: Philosophy and Goals."

[37] LaPolt, Alisa. "Private Groups Profit from W-2 Agencies Criticized for Taking Funds." *Wisconsin State Journal.* November 19, 1998, 1B.

[38] Ibid.

[39] Ibid.

[40] Cole, Jeff. "Lacking Money, 'Seinfeld' Suit Victor Leaving Town, As Appeal Plays Out, Ex-Miller Fanatic Laments Trouble Finding Work." *Milwaukee Journal Sentinel*. October 26, 1998, 5.

[41] Segall, Cary. "'Seinfeld! Firing Case on Agenda at Issue Whether Companies Must Tell Employees of Decisions That Affect Their Jobs." *Wisconsin State Journal*. November 25, 2000, A1.

[42] Ibid.

[43] Chaptman, Dennis. "$24.7 Million 'Seinfeld' Verdict Rejected Again." *Milwaukee Journal Sentinel*. March 21, 2001, 1A.

[44] Beauchamp, Tom L., and Norman E. Bowie, eds. *Ethical Theory and Business*. Upper Saddle River: Prentice Hall, 2001, 267.

[45] Kuske, 3.

[46] Phillips, David, and Mark Truby. "Car Firms Insure Same-Sex Partners." *Detroit News*. June 9, 2000, A01.

[47] Biers, John M., "TP Offers Partner Benefits to Same-Sex Partners More Companies Adopting New Policy." *Times-Picayune*. October 3, 2001, C1.

[48] Phillips and Truby.

[49] Price, Deb. "Big 3 Smooth Out the Ride to Equality." *Detroit News*. June 19, 2000, A11.

[50] Phillips and Truby.

[51] "City Establishes Gay Registry." *Wisconsin State Journal*. July 14, 1999, 3C.

[52] Goldberg, Carey. "Gay Couples in Vermont Joined in 'Civil Union.'" *Milwaukee Journal Sentinel*. July 2, 2000, 11 5A.

[53] Wade, Nicholas. "Clinton Seeks Study on Ethics of Cell Work President Wants 'Thorough Review' of Research at UW-Madison, Elsewhere." *Milwaukee Journal Sentinel*. November 15, 1998.

[54] Holland, Judy. "Scientists Fear the Loss of Stem Cell Funds." *Milwaukee Journal Sentinel*. January 15, 2001, 1A.

[55] Ibid.

[56] Richardson, John E., ed. *Business Ethics*. Sluice Dock: McGraw-Hill, 1999, 138.

[57] Ibid.

[58] Hawkins Jr., Lee. "Executive Gets Salary Guarantee." *Milwaukee Journal Sentinel*. January 15, 2001, 3D.

[59] Chilsen, Jim. "Pabst Getting No Blue Ribbons at Home." *Houston Chronicle*. September 15, 1996, 12.

[60] Schultz, Ellen E. "Raw Deals: Companies Quietly Use Mergers and Spin-Offs to Cut Worker Benefits—Even as They Pump Up Pension-Plan Surpluses, Employers Slash Payouts—Ms. Jastram Can't Even Make Rent." *Wall Street Journal*. December 27, 2000, A1.

[61] Weintraub, Joanne. "Sex, Belize and Videotape." *Milwaukee Journal Sentinel*. January 8, 2001, 1A.

[62] Clarkson, Kenneth, Roger LeRoy Miller, Gaylord A. Jentz, and Frank B. Cross, eds. "Case 32.4—In re Johns Manville Corp." *West's Business Law*. West: n.p., 1998, 570.

[63] Wermiel, Stephen. "Supreme Court Rules Union Pacts May Be Ignored Under Chapter 11—Decision a Blow to Labor, Seen Helping Companies in Bankruptcy Courts." *Wall Street Journal*. February 23, 1984, 1.

[64] Bernstein, Harry. "Cooperative Experiment May Not Be Deed." *Los Angeles Times*. July 2, 1986, 1.

[65] Dresang, Joel. "Advocates Press Firstar to Help Out-of-Work Laborers." *Milwaukee Journal Sentinel*. January 16, 2001, 2D.

[66] Mintz, M. "The Dangers Insurance Companies Hide." *Washington Monthly*. 23 (1/2): 38.

[67] Clarkson, 571.

RESEARCH RESOURCES

Adams, David M., and Maine, Edward W. *Business Ethics for the 21st Century*. Mayfield: Mountain View, 1998.

Administration for Children and Families. "ACF: News and Facts." Washington, DC: US Department of Health and Human Services, 2001. Address: www.acf.dhhs.gov/news/facts/tanf.html. Accessed July 1, 2003.

Aquinas, Thomas. *Summa of the Summa*. Ed. Peter Kreeft. San Francisco: Ignatius Press, 1990.

Aron, Leon. "The Death of Soviet Control." *The American Enterprise*. 11 (2000) 1:38-45.

AG Edwards Inc. "Annual Report Fiscal Year 2001." Address: www.agedwards.com/annualrpt/ar01/index.html. Accessed June 15, 2003.

Bachman, S.L. "The Political Economy of Child Labor and Its Impacts on International Business." *Business Economics*. 35 (2000) 3:30-41.

Beauchamp, Tom L., and Bowie, Norman E., ed. *Ethical Theory and Business*. Upper Saddle River: Prentice Hall, 2001.

Behm, Don; Borsuk, Alan Borusk; and Hawkins, Lee. "Mining Proposal Gets Cold Reception Across State in Green Bay, Milwaukee; Foes Say Mine Could Hurt Environment." *Milwaukee Journal Sentinel*. February 18, 1997, 1.

Bernstein, Harry. "Cooperative Experiments May Not Be Dead." *Los Angeles Times*. July 2, 1986, 1.

Berthelsen, Christian. "How Energy Giant Tried to Cut a Deal/Duke Inc. Offered to Reduce Bill If State Halted Probes." *San Francisco Chronicle*. May 3, 2001, A4.

Biers, John M. "TP Offers Partner Benefits to Same-Sex Partners; More Companies Adopting New Policy." *Times-Picayune*. October 3, 2001, C1.

Borowski, Greg. "Council Oks Lead Paint Lawsuit." *Milwaukee Journal Sentinel*. October 20, 2000, 1B.

Borsuk, Alan J. "Kids May Pay for City's High Rate of Single Moms: Where 60% of Mothers Are Single, Children Are Left with a Murky Future." *Milwaukee Journal Sentinel*. July 3, 2002, 1A.

Boyes, William, and Melvin, Michael. *Economics*. Boston: Houghton Mifflin Co, 1999.

Brandt, Walther I., ed. *Luther's Works*. Philadelphia: Muhlenberg Press, 1962.

Bureau of Labor Information and Customer Service. "Milwaukee County Workforce Profile." Wisconsin Department of Workforce Development. DWEI-10633-P. December, 2000: 1-7.

Bureau of Labor Statistics. "Consumer Expenditure in 1999." United States Department of Labor. Address: stats.bls.gov/csxashar.htm#1999. Accessed July 15, 2001.

Bustillo, Miguel; Reiterman, Tim; and Landsberg, Mitchell. "California and the West; The California Energy Crisis; Capitol Blame Game Frays Bipartisanship; GOP Lawmakers Criticize PUC at Assemble Hearing; The Party Plans Radio Ads Attacking Governor. Democrats Target Past Republican Leaders." *Los Angeles Times*. February 8, 2001, A3.

Ceniceros, Roberto. "Employers, Health Plans Trying Various Remedies for Soaring Drug Costs." *Business Insurance*. June 30, 2003.

Chaptman, Dennis. "$24.7 Million 'Seinfeld' Verdict Rejected Again." *Milwaukee Journal Sentinel*. March 21, 2001, 1A.

Chatterjee, Sumana, and Sudarsan, Raghavan. "Bitter Trail: Who's Responsible for Labor Atrocities." *Milwaukee Journal Sentinel.* June 24, 2001, 8D.

Chewing, Richard, ed. *Biblical Principles and Economics: The Foundations.* Colorado Springs: NavPress, 1989.

Chilsen, Jim. "Pabst Getting No Blue Ribbons at Home." *Houston Chronicle.* September 15, 1996, 12.

"City Establishes Gay Registry." *Wisconsin State Journal.* July 14, 1999, 3C.

Clarkson, Kenneth; Miller, Roger LeRoy; Jentz, Gaylord A.; and Cross, Frank B. eds. "Case 32.4: In re Johns Manville Corp." *West's Business Law.* 7th edition, West Educational Publishing: 1998.

Cole, Jeff. "Lacking Money, 'Seinfeld' Suit Victor Leaving Town as Appeal Plays Out; Ex-Miller Fanatic Laments Trouble Finding Work." *Milwaukee Journal Sentinel.* October 26, 1998, 5.

Congress, Senate. Governmental Affairs Committee. "Senate Hearings on Sweepstakes." 106th Congress. 1st Session. March 10, 1999.

Deutsch, Anthony. "Mercy Killings." *Milwaukee Journal Sentinel.* April 11, 2001, 5A.

Department of Workforce Development. "Wisconsin Works: Philosophy and Goals." Address: www.dwd.state.wi.us/desw2/philosop.htm. Accessed June 18, 2001.

Di Norcia, Vincent. *Hard Like Water.* Oxford University Press: Toronto, 1999.

Dresang, Joel. "Advocates Press Firstar to Help Out-of-Work Laborers." *Milwaukee Journal Sentinel.* January 16, 2001, 2D.

Ecumenical Task Force of the Niagara Frontier. "Background on the Love Canal." University Archives, University Libraries, State University of New York at Buffalo, Address: ublib.buffalo.edu/libraries/projects/lovecanal/background_lovecanal.html. Accessed June 18, 2001.

Elliott, John D. "Disintegration of the Soviet Politico-Economic System." *International Journal of Social Economics*. 22 (1995) 3:31-61.

Ellwanger, Rev. Joseph W. "Letter to the Editor: Partnership Registry Good for City." *Milwaukee Journal Sentinel*. July 11, 1999.

"Exxon, Toyota, GM to Join on Fuel Cell." *Milwaukee Journal Sentinel*. January 2, 2001, 1D.

Federal Trade Commission. "FTC Matter No. 001-0174: FTC Issues Report on Midwest Gasoline Price Investigation." Washington, DC: Federal Trade Commission, March 29, 2001. Address: www.ftc.gov/opa/2001/03/midwest.htm. Accessed May 31, 2001.

Flasch, Jim. "The Crandon Mine and Northeast WI." *Marketplace Magazine*. December 10, 1996.

Frontline. "Blackout." PBS. June 2001. Address: www.pbs.org/wgbh/pages/frontline/shows/blackout/. Accessed June 18, 2001.

General Motors Corp. "2003 Annual Report." Address: www.gm.com/company/investor_information/docs/fin_data/gm03ar/index.html. Accessed May 17, 2006.

Goldberg, Carey. "Gay Couples in Vermont Joined in 'Civil Union.'" *Milwaukee Journal Sentinel*. July 2, 2000, 16A.

Griffin, Kawanza. "City Ranks Poorly on Teen Births." *Milwaukee Journal Sentinel*. January 26, 2003, 2G.

Hajewski, Doris. "The Unsettling Price of Low-Cost Clothes." *Milwaukee Journal Sentinel*. December 31, 2000, 11A.

Hartman, Laur Pincus, ed. *Perspectives in Business Ethics.* Boston: McGraw Hill, 1998.

Hauter, Wenonah, and Slocum, Tyson. "It's Greed Stupid! Debunking the Ten Myths of Utility Deregulation." *Public Citizen Critical Mass Energy and Environment Program.* January 2001: 1-17.

Hawkins, Lee. "Key to a Turnaround." *Milwaukee Journal Sentinel.* August 28, 2000. 15D.

Hawkins Jr., Lee. "Executive Gets Salary Guarantee." *Milwaukee Journal Sentinel.* January 15, 2001, 3D.

Hoffman, Michael W.; Frederick, Robert E.; and Schwartz, Mark S. eds. *Business Ethics: Readings and Cases in Corporate Morality.* Boston: McGraw Hill: 2001.

Holland, Judy. "Scientists Fear the Loss of Stem Cell Funds." *Milwaukee Journal Sentinel.* January 15, 2001, 1A.

Holzer, Harry J. "Career Advancement Prospects and Strategies for Low-Wage Minority Workers." *Low-Wage Workers in the New Economy.* Ed. Richard Kazis and Marc S. Miller. Washington, DC: The Urban Institute Press, 2001.

International Programme on the Elimination of Child Labour. "Every Child Counts: New Estimates on Child Labor." International Labour Office. Geneva, Switzerland: International Labor Organization, 2002.

Jones, Meg. "State's Sweepstakes Trial Gets Under Way." *Milwaukee Journal Sentinel.* November 2, 2000, 1B.

Kay, John. "Staking a Moral Claim. (Proposal for a Social Market Perspective on Economics)." *New Statesman.* October 11, 1996, 18-21.

Kaye, Stephen H. "Improved Employment Opportunities for People with Disabilities." Washington, DC: National Institute on Disability and Rehabilitation Research. United States Department of Education, 2003, 1-49.

Kudrov, Valentin. "The Comparison of the USSR and USA Economies by IMEMO in the 1970s." *Europe-Asia Studies.* 49 (1997) 5:883-905.

Kuske, David. *Luther's Catechism.* Milwaukee: Northwestern Publishing House, 1998.

LaPolt, Alisa. "Private Groups Profit from W-2 Agencies Criticized for Taking Funds." *Wisconsin State Journal.* November 19, 1998, 1B.

Legislative Reference Bureau. "Highlights of State and Local Finances in Wisconsin." *2005–2006 Wisconsin Bluebook.* Madison, WI: Joint Committee on Legislative Organization, 2005.

—————————————. "Wisconsin Adjusted Gross Income by County, 1991–1995." *1997–1998 Wisconsin Bluebook.* Madison, WI: Legislative Reference Bureau, 1999.

McNeil, John. "Disability." Washington, DC: United States Census Bureau, 2001. Address: www.census.gov/population/www/popuprofile/disabil.html. Accessed May 30, 2006.

Michele, Tom. "Impact of Proposed Crandon Mine Explained." *Rhinelander Daily News,* April 4, 1995, 1.

Millard, Johnson. "The Checks and Balances in Pursuing the Crandon Mine." *Corporate Report Wisconsin.* August 1, 1997.

Miller, D.W. "Sweatshop Protest Ends at U of Michigan." *The Chronicle of Higher Education.* April 2, 1999, A46.

"Millennium 2000: Environment." January 2, 2000: Address: www.cnn.com/TRANSCRIPTS/0001/02/se.35.html. Accessed July 5, 2001.

Millman, Joel. "Fortune Brands Moves Units to Mexico to Lower Costs, Some of America's Most Recognized Products Are Made South of the Border." *Wall Street Journal.* August 7, 2001, B2.

Milwaukee Board of Fire and Police Commissioners. "City of Milwaukee 2001 Public Safety Report." Address: www.milwaukee.gov/fpc/2001PSR.pdf. Accessed June 13, 2003.

"Minorities as % of Total Population, by Community." *Milwaukee Journal Sentinel.* Address: www2.jsonline.com/news/census2000/mar01/minorities03091gx.asp. Accessed May 30, 2006.

Mintz, M. "The Dangers Insurance Companies Hide." *Washington Monthly.* Jan/Feb 1991.

Muhm, Don. *The NFO: A Farm Belt Rebel: The History of the National Farm Organization.* Rochester, MN: Lone Oak Press, 2000.

National Agricultural Statistics Service. "Wisconsin: Farm Numbers and Land in Farms." Address: www.nass.usda.gov/. Accessed May 30, 2006.

"1999 Residential Sales: District 17." City of Milwaukee: Assessor's Office. Address: www.ci.mil.wi.us/citygov/assessor/99dist17.htm. Accessed January 3, 2001.

Nixon, Robert. "Students Protest 'Sweatshops' Outside of Kohl's." *Westchester County Business Journal.* October 23, 2000, 8.

Norris, Floyd. "Auditors Have a Responsibility to Call Sham Profits What They Are." *Milwaukee Journal Sentinel.* May 20, 2001, 3D.

Office of Economic Advisors. "2000–2001 Affirmative Action for Milwaukee County. Wisconsin Department of Workforce Development. Address: www.dwd.state.wi.us/dwelmi/aa_pdf/Milwaukee.pdf. Accessed June 18, 2001.

Office of Management and Budget. "Table 22–1. Budget Authority by Function, Category, and Program/FY2002." Executive Office of the President. Address: www.whitehouse.gov/omb/budget/fy2002/bud22_1.html. Accessed July 15, 2001.

Office of National Drug Control Policy. "The Economic Costs of Alcohol and Drug Abuse in the United States: 1992–1998, No. 190636." Washington, DC: Executive Office of the President, 2001, 1-85.

——————————————. "National Drug Control Budget Executive Summary, Fiscal Year 2002." Washington, DC: Executive Office of the President, April 9, 2001, 1-8.

Olmstead, Alan, and Rhode, Paul W. "The Transformation of Northern Agriculture, 1910–1990." *The Cambridge Economic History of the United States: Volume 3*. Ed. Stanley L. Engerman and Robert E. Gallman. Cambridge: Cambridge University Press, 2001.

Pabst, Georgia. "Purple Passions Colorful Building Angers Some Business Neighbors." *Milwaukee Journal Sentinel*. January 7, 2001, 1B.

Phillips, David, and Truby, Mark. "Car Firms Insure Same-Sex Partners It's Biggest Extension of Benefits to Gays by a Single Industry." *Detroit News*. June 9, 2000, A01.

Post, James E.; Lawrence, Anne T; and Weber, James. *Business and Society*. Boston: Irwin-McGraw-Hill, 1999.

Price, Deb. "Big 3 Smooth Out the Ride to Equality." *Detroit News*. June 19, 2000, A11.

Rast, Joel. "Transportation Equity and Access to Jobs." UW-Milwaukee Center for Economic Development, 2004: 1-33.

Rector, Robert. "The Effects of Welfare Reform." *Heritage Foundation*. March 15, 2001. Address: www.heritage.org/Research/Welfare/Test031501b.cfm, Accessed July 1, 2003.

Reich, Robert. "The New Meaning of Corporate Social Responsibility." *California Management Review*. 40 (1998) 2:8-18.

Richardson, John E. ed. *Business Ethics*. Sluice Dock: Dushkin/McGraw Hill, 1999.

Ross, Michael E. "It Seemed Like a Good Idea at the Time." Address: www.MSNBC.MSN.com/id/7209828/. Accessed May 30, 2006.

Romell, Rick. "Big Investor Seeks Change for Gehl: Florida Man Urges West Bend Firm to Sell Farm Equipment Division." *Milwaukee Journal Sentinel*. June 12, 1997, 1.

Rose, Craig D. "Only a Few Bad Apples? Despite Reforms, Investors Haven't Seen the Last of Corporate Greed." *San Diego Union-Tribune*. May 4, 2003, H1.

Sabo, Congressman Martin. "How Uncle Sam Could Help to Address the Income Gap." Address: Sabo.house.gov. Accessed May 30, 2006.

Sacks, Jonathan. "Markets and Morals." *First Things: A Monthly Journal of Religion and Public Life*. August 2000, 23-32.

Savage, Mark. "Master Lock Employees Squeezed Between Costs and Profits. Some Workers Doubt Need to Move Work South, Are Unhappy with Union." *Milwaukee Journal Sentinel*. September 26, 1999, 3.

Schlosser, Eric. "The Business of Pornography: Most of the Outsize Profits Being Generated by Pornography Today Are Being Earned by Businesses Not Traditionally Associated with the Sex Industry." *US News and World Report*. February 10, 1997, 42-51.

Schultz, Ellen E. "Raw Deals: Companies Quietly Use Mergers and Spinoffs to Cut Worker Benefits, Even as They Pump Up Pension-Plan Surpluses, Employers Slash Payouts, Ms. Jastram Can't Even Make Rent." *Wall Street Journal*. December 27, 2000, A1.

Segall, Cary. "'Seinfeld' Firing Case on Agenda at Issue Whether Companies Must Tell Employees of Decision That Affect Their Jobs." *Wisconsin State Journal*. November 25, 2000, 1A.

Slavin, Stephan L. *Macroeconomics 4th Edition*. Chicago: Irwin, 1996.

Smith, Adam. *An Inquiry into the Nature and Causes of the Wealth of Nations.* New York: The Modern Library, 1937.

Smith, Adam. *The Theory of Moral Sentiments.* Indianapolis: Liberty Classics, 1976.

Smith, Rebecca. "Power Deregulation: A Year Later Most Players Think the New System Works." *San Francisco Chronicle.* March 31, 1999, B1.

Sorking, Andrew Ross. "Putting 'Hostile' Back into Takeover." *New York Times.* February 25, 2001, BU1.

"The US Pays Up—Finally." *Milwaukee Journal Sentinel.* February 12, 2001. Address: www.jsonline.com. Accessed May 31, 2001.

Theiberger, Frederic. *King Solomon.* London: Horowitz Publishing, 1947.

Tokic, Damir. "What Went Wrong with the Dot-Coms?" *Journal of Investing.* 11 (2002) 2:52-57.

Unger, Ray. "Anatomy of a Stock Market Hiccup." *Madison Capital Times.* November 4, 1997, 1C1.

United States Conference of Catholic Bishops. "Economic Justice for All: Catholic Social Teaching and the U.S. Economy." *National Catholic Reporter.* January 9, 1987.

United States Census Bureau. "County Estimates for People of All Ages in Poverty for Wisconsin: 1997." Address: www.census.gov/hhes/www/saipe/stcty/a97_55.htm. Accessed January 3, 2001.

—————————————. "Income, Poverty, and Health Insurance Coverage in the United States, 2003." Washington, DC: Government Printing Office, 2004.

—————————————. "State and County Quick Facts: Milwaukee County, Wisconsin." Address: quickfacts.census.gov/cgi-bin/county?cnty=55079. Accessed January 3, 2001.

———————. "USA Counties 1998—Poverty: Forest County, Wisconsin." Address: censtats.census.gov/cgi-bin/usac/usatable.pl. Accessed April 24, 2000.

Vanden Brook, Tom. "Company Developing Crandon Mine Offers New Environmental Safeguards." *Milwaukee Journal Sentinel*. December 9, 1998, 1.

Wade, Nicholas. "Clinton Seeks Study on Ethics of Cell Work President Wants 'Thorough Review' of Research at UW-Madison, Elsewhere." *Milwaukee Journal Sentinel*. November 15, 1998.

Weintraub, Joanne. "Sex, Belize and Videotape." *Milwaukee Journal Sentinel*. January 9, 2001, 1A.

Wermiel, Stephen. "Supreme Court Rules Union Pacts May Be Ignored under Chapter 11: Decision a Blow to Labor, Seen Helping Companies in Bankruptcy Courts." *Wall Street Journal*. February 23, 1984, 1.

Will, Lester. "Economic Divide Growing, Poll Finds Many Feel." *Milwaukee Journal Sentinel*. June 22, 2001, 9A.

Wisconsin Department of Public Instruction. "2000–2001 Graduation Final Publication Report." Address: www2.dpi.state.wi.us/spr/grad.asp. Accessed June 13, 2003.

Wisconsin Department of Workforce Development. "Forest County Workforce Profile." Division of Workforce Excellence. Bureau of Workforce Information. July 1999.

Wiseman, Michael. "In the Midst of Reform: Wisconsin in 1997: ANF Discussion Paper 99–03." Washington, DC: The Urban Institute, 1999.

Yue Jones, Terril. "Ford." *Milwaukee Journal Sentinel*. May 29, 2001, 1D.

Zahn, Mary. "Waiting for a Check That Doesn't Arrive Elderly Sure That They Had Won End Up Drained of Cash, Dreams Swept Up in Sweepstakes." *Milwaukee Journal Sentinel*. March 14, 1999, 1.

I'm a Christian Even at Work—Bible Study by Jerry L. Poppe, **22N1139.** This Bible study, correlated with the book, is available online. The study includes teacher's guide and student lesson copy masters. Seven lessons. It is obtainable as an RTF sent electronically via e-mail. Order from www.nph.net or 1-800-662-6022.